BLACK COUNTRY
Memories 2

To

Norman

Best wishes

Merry Christmas

Front cover top: *A cracking shot of children enjoying VE Day in Gordon Street, Wolverhampton.*
Front cover bottom: *Miners at work.*
Back cover: *Chainmakers at work.*

BLACK COUNTRY
Memories 2

CARL CHINN

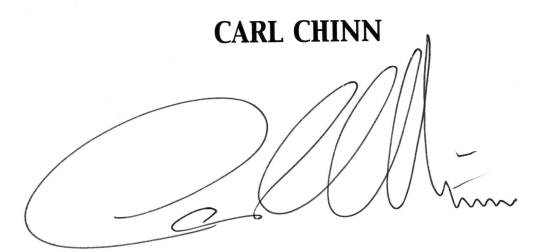

BREWIN BOOKS

First published by
Brewin Books Ltd, 56 Alcester Road,
Studley, Warwickshire B80 7LG in 2005
www.brewinbooks.com

ISBN 1 85858 279 2

A Cataloguing in Publication Record
for this title is available from the British Library.

Typeset in Times
Printed in Great Britain by
The Alden Press

CONTENTS

ACKNOWLEDGEMENTS

It is a thrill to be writing a local history feature for the *Express and Star*. The paper is not only the biggest-selling evening newspaper in the country outside London, but also it is marked out by its commitment to its region and the people of that region. There can be few papers that are as local as the *Express and Star* and that commitment to localness affects positively every aspect of its reporting and coverage. The Black Country is fortunate to have a paper so dedicated to the well being of Black Country folk. I thank the editor of the *Express and Star*, Adrian Faber, and its management for giving me the opportunity to write so extensively about the Black Country. Adrian has been a constant source of support and encouragement to me and like me is a proud West Midlander. My appreciation is also due to Charlie Moss, Adrian's secretary, who carefully and thoughtfully collects all the memories and photos sent in to me; Graeme Andrew and Dave Hotchkiss the news sub-editors, who put together my pages in such a talented and sensitive way; and Mark Green, internet information control officer, who has played an important role in sourcing photographs. I also thank the readers of the *Express and Star* who have honoured me by sharing with me their memories and letting me see their photos and precious memorabilia.

FOREWORD

Carl Chinn is a modern day wonder. On the one hand, a serious historian with a vast knowledge of the heritage of the West Midlands. On the other hand, a human whirlwind whose energy and enthusiasm is breathtaking.

His understanding of the West Midlands is second to none. It has been a privilege and a pleasure to have him as part of the Express & Star team. His regular articles are undoubtedly one of the most popular parts of the paper. His legions of fans recognise the depth of knowledge he brings to his subject. He is a writer who has that rare talent of bringing the true human story to the vast breadth of history.

Oddly enough, Carl and myself have followed a similar path in the early part of our lives - growing up in the same part of Birmingham, going to the same secondary school and both attending Birmingham University. Now two Brummies have been reunited in the Black Country.

This is the second of our Black Country Memories books. The first was a sell-out. I shall never forget the queues of people in our front office waiting to tell Carl their stories and have their books signed. It was like a rugby scrum!

I am sure you will enjoy this new volume. It tells the stories of the people and places that have made the Black Country and the West Midlands the great powerhouse of Britain. The articles are sometimes funny and sometimes touching, but never dull.

Carl - thanks, mate.

Adrian Faber

Editor, Express & Star

Black Country Memories

I dedicate this to the people of the Black Country who have kept alive our dialect and whose hard work was vital in making England the greatest manufacturing nation in the world.

Chapter 1

HEARTFELT CELEBRATIONS: VICTORY IN EUROPE

In the long history of England, Scotland and Wales there had never been such heartfelt celebrations like those that greeted Victory in Europe Day on 8 May 1945. Tens of thousands of street parties brought millions of people out of their homes to join with their kin and neighbours in joyfully acclaiming peace and the end of a bitter, remorseless conflict that had threatened the very being of the nation.

On two outstanding occasions before, our land had been swept with a mood of thanksgiving, relief and happiness that powerful foreign enemies had been defeated and that an invasion had been staved off. The first of these was in 1588. In the summer of that year great bonfires had been lit from the English Channel to the Scottish borders and from the Irish Sea to the North Sea to warn of the approach of the Spanish Armada.

Sent by Philip II to punish England for its resolute independence of action and for siding with Spain's enemies, this was one of the biggest and best-organised fleets that had ever put to sea. Made up of 130 galleons, merchantmen, galleys and various small craft, it boasted 10,000 sailors and 20,000 tough soldiers belonging to the greatest empire in the Western world.

Sighted off the Lizard on the evening 19 July, the Armada posed a formidable threat, but over the next few weeks and through a combination of fierce winds, heavy seas and dogged attacks by English 'sea dogs' such as Hawkins, Frobisher and Drake, that mighty gathering of ships was broken up and half of it was destroyed.

The defeat of the Spanish Armada was regarded as almost miraculous by the English and was greeted with an enthusiasm deeply affected by religious sentiment. Church bells pealed, huzzahs were shouted, bonfires were lit now in delight and pride and not fear, and Queen Elizabeth I ordered that various medals be struck to commemorate the remarkable victory. One of them was inscribed with the Latin words "Afflavit Deus et dissipantur" - "God blew with his breath, and they were scattered".

England, and this time Britain as well, faced a second fearsome threat to its existence in 1805. Led by Napoleon Bonaparte, one of history's most successful generals, the French armies had defeated all who had stood against them in Europe.

Napoleon then resolved to invade Britain, the most defiant and determined enemy of France. From late 1803, he gathered at Boulogne 2,000 flat-bottomed boats, which were to transport his 100,000 strong army across the English Channel. But this could not be done until the British blockade of French ports was lifted and the threat of the Royal Navy was removed.

On 19 October 1805 and in pursuit of his aims, Napoleon ordered the combined French and Spanish fleet to leave the port of Cadiz in Spain. Two days later battle was joined at Trafalgar. The British were led by the legendary Nelson, the nation's most celebrated naval hero who had already won notable victories over the French. Out of 33 ships, the enemy lost eighteen and a momentous triumph had been gained. But celebrations in Britain were muted by Nelson's death from wounds just after he was told of his success.

Word of the "glorious yet melancholy" victory reached the West Midlands from Plymouth on 11 November, when the only paper locally, *Aris's Birmingham Gazette*, carried this notice:

> Never was the victorious banner so darkened and discoloured as this has been by the death of the glorious and intrepid Chief, through whose skilful arrangements, aided by congenial spirits, the conquest was achieved. This fell discord marred the general harmony of opinion. Every man smiled at the great news of victory; but when the price was told the *smile* was followed by a *sigh*. The general sensation was one of gladness chastened by sorrow, such as it has never before been our lot to witness. The bells were rang with clangs of joy, but those demonstrations of triumph were again softened by the mournful peal of muffled bells. The inhabitants did not illuminate their houses upon this occasion, because the hero ... was no more!

The Battle of Trafalgar was as vital as the Battle of Britain of 1940 in saving this nation from tyranny, but the tragic loss of Nelson meant that the end of the threat of a French invasion was not greeted with the same delight that infused every Briton on Tuesday 8 May 1945, Victory in Europe Day.

In fact the war in Europe had ended the day before, when Admiral Doenitz had announced the unconditional surrender of all German fighting troops. Doenitz had become Fuhrer on 1 May when German radio had announced that Hitler had "fallen this afternoon at his command post in the Reich Chancellery (in Berlin), fighting to the last breath against Bolshevism and for Germany". Formerly the commander of all U-boat operations, Doenitz had become Grand Admiral and Commander-in-Chief of German naval forces in 1943.

Regarded as a ruthless foe, in the broadcast announcing his leadership he vowed to "save the German people from destruction from Bolshevists" and declared that "as long as the British and Americans hamper us from reaching this end we shall fight and defend ourselves against them as well".

Thankfully, Doenitz failed. Germany's forces were in full retreat and its power was waning rapidly. In Italy, Mussolini, the fascist leader and ally of Hitler, had been executed by partisans on 29 April, the same day that the German Army there had surrendered to Field Marshall Alexander. This surrender was effective from 2 May, on which date British troops entered Lubeck in northern Germany, thereby reaching the Baltic and the Red Army. Then on 5 May, Field Marshall Montgomery accepted at Luneburg Heath the German surrender in North Germany, Holland and Denmark.

To the east, the Russian Red Army had captured Berlin and was advancing remorselessly. Nazi Germany was soon to be destroyed and Doenitz could not hold off defeat. Within days of taking over from Hitler, he had

The flags are already out in Market Street, Wolverhampton on 7 May in anticipation of the end of the war in Europe.

ordered all German U-boats to cease hostilities and return to their bases. This was reported early on the morning of 7 May. That afternoon, the Danish Home Service, once again run by Danes and not Nazis, stated that the German forces in Norway had surrendered.

A few hours later, Count Schwerin von Krosigk, who had recently been made foreign minister, announced an unconditional surrender by the Germans, although it was later reported that German troops in Czechoslovakia intended to fight to the last. Despite this, by late afternoon news of the German surrender was spreading across Europe – but still no official confirmation came.

In Britain there was an air of taut expectancy, as if folk could not yet dare to hope that the end of the long and hard war was indeed nigh. The town centres of the Black Country and Birmingham were busier than usual, as folk gathered cautiously to await the news that they prayed for. Disappointment covered many faces, although a lightening of lines brought to the fore the expectation of peace.

Still as the day went on and it seemed more and more likely that the war was over, Union Flags and some flags of the Allies began to be flown from shops and other business premises. Even so, no official news came and at 4.45 p.m. Supreme Headquarters authorised correspondents to make it clear that no official statement had as yet been made concerning the complete surrender of all German armed forces in Europe. A few minutes later, an American reporter said that Winston Churchill, Prime Minister of the United Kingdom, and Harry Truman, President of the United States of America had intended to announce VE Day at 6 p.m., but that it had been postponed because Marshall Stalin, leader of the Soviet Union (Russia), was not ready.

Queues of people lined up to buy papers from sellers in the streets. Indeed, many vendors were swamped so soon as ever they left the newspaper offices. Notwithstanding the delay in proclaiming VE Day, the evening papers were proclaiming that the Germans had surrendered. Encouraged by these positive reports, by night time people were casting off their tension and were beginning to believe that an official announcement was imminent. Groups came together and paraded up and down the main streets, singing patriotic songs, hymns and popular songs. Away from the town centres, many householders freed themselves from the blackout and switched on the lights inside and outside their homes where possible.

The next morning, 8 May, papers at last carried the news that it was "VE Day Today". Because newsprint was in short supply and rationed, coming as it did from paper mills in Canada and Sweden, newspapers had to cut back on the size of their

A bonfire on VE night at Lyde Green, Cradley.

A cracking shot of children enjoying VE Day in Gordon Street, Wolverhampton.

papers. Many were limited to just four pages of broadsheet size. They reported that at 3 p.m. Mr Churchill was to broadcast the news that the war in Europe was at an end. The Ministry of Information communiqué added that 8 and 9 May would be public holidays and that the King was to broadcast to the Empire and Commonwealth at 9 p.m. that evening.

As ever, Churchill was stirring. He explained that hostilities would end officially at one minute after midnight on VE Day, but a Cease Fire had begun the day before so as to save lives – whilst "our dear Channel Islands are also to be freed today". In some places German troops were continuing to fight the Red Army, but at 2.41 a.m. on Monday the Germans had signed the act of unconditional surrender "of all German land, sea and air forces in Europe to the Allied Expeditionary Force and simultaneously to the Soviet High Command".

The Prime Minister stressed that 'today, perhaps, we shall think mostly of ourselves. Tomorrow we shall pay a particular tribute to our Russian comrades, whose prowess in the field has been one of the grand contributions to the general victory. Churchill brought to the fore the fact that:

after gallant France had been struck down we maintained the struggle single-handed for a whole year until we were joined by Soviet Russia and, later, by the overwhelming power and resources of the United States of America. Finally, almost the whole world was combined against the evil-doers who are now prostate before us. Our gratitude to our splendid Allies goes forth from all our hearts in this island and throughout the British Empire.

We may allow ourselves a brief period of rejoicing, but let us not forget for as moment the toil and efforts that lie ahead. Japan, with all her treachery and greed, remains unsubdued. The injury she has inflicted on Great Britain, the United States and other countries, and her detestable cruelties, call for justice and retribution.

We must now devote all our strength and resources to the completion of our task, both at home and abroad. Advance Britannia! Long live the cause of freedom! God save the King!"

As that greatest of all English orators finished his exhortation, buglers of the Scots Guards sounded the 'Cease Fire'. Churchill then went to the House of Commons to make the same speech, after which he added his

Residents in Sutherland Place, Wolverhampton preparing to burn an effigy of Hitler on a bonfire on VE Day.

deep gratitude to the House "which has proved itself the strongest foundation for waging war that has ever been seen in the whole of our long history". The strength of Parliamentary institutions had been able to both "preserve all the title deeds of democracy while waging war in the most stern and protracted form". The Prime Minster then moved that the House of Commons should attend the Church of Saint Margaret, Westminster "to give humble and reverent thanks to Almighty God for our deliverance from the threat of German domination".

A victory party for the children of Pope Road, The Scotlands, Wolverhampton on 14 May 1945 in the surface shelter in Masefield Road Church. The Reverend H. S. Light, minister of Low Hill Congregational Church, is saying grace before the youngsters tuck in.

Later that afternoon, Churchill drove from Downing Street to Buckingham Palace. Smoking his trademark cigar, he was rapturously cheered by throngs of people to which he waved and made his famous V for Victory sign. He then appeared with the Royal Family on the balcony of the palace. When he left, the crowd cheered him and sang, "For He's a Jolly Good Fellow". Three times in three hours, King George V, Queen Elizabeth and Princesses Elizabeth and Margaret had to go out to the balcony to receive the acclaim of the huge crowds; and in between the two young princesses also mingled with the exultant host.

In the West Midlands, as elsewhere VE Day was marked by the pealing of church bells, the relaying by loudspeakers of the king's broadcast speech at 9 p.m., parades of Civil Defence organisations and, of course, street parties. Overnight men and women had happily hung up bunting and flags, and it seemed that the poorer the neighbourhood the more colourful and plentiful were the decorations that garlanded the streets. As the preparations were made, they were accompanied by the bangs of fireworks that some people with foresight had saved from before the war – for there had been no public sale of fireworks for six years.

The day itself was a damp one, but not even the rain could mar the cheerfulness that abounded. Because of the bad weather, some parties took place in school halls or such like, but most were held in the street. And in many places, these parties had been planned for months.

Once the Battle of Normandy had been won in 1944 and it seemed that victory would come, the women who organised the charabanc trips for a street and the chaps who helped them had started to collect money from their neighbours, along with whatever food anyone could spare. It wasn't easy in a time of rationing, but folks gave what they could, living as they did in a world where sharing was a way of life. So here and there were a couple of spoonfuls of sugar or tea, a packet of custard or jelly, and perhaps even the odd food coupon.

Working-class neighbourhoods had plenty of people skilled in arranging celebrations, having had experience with the Armistice Day parties of 1918 and with the silver jubilee celebrations of 1935 and the Coronation parties of 1937. So whilst some observers were surprised at how well organised the street parties were, there was no surprise to those who lived locally.

And many's the street where youngsters were given mementoes or Bibles and where they enjoyed themselves in fancy dress and games. And then, when the childrens' events were over, the pianos were brought out, the sing-songs began and the bonfires were lit – many of which boasted effigies of Hitler.

But whatever the celebrations, VE Day was also a time of commemoration for those who had died, those were scarred physically or mentally by war, those who were bereaved. This VE Day anniversary, then, let us celebrate Britain's great victory over Nazism and the triumph of good over evil but let us also commemorate those whose sacrifices gave us our freedom and let us recall that for many the war was not over. The Forgotten Army continued to battle against the Japanese for over three more months and now more than ever they should not be forgotten. And let us also realise that for many still living they continue to carry with them the sorrows caused by the Second World War. Most of all, let those of us who have lived in peace pledge to those who fought and worked for our liberties that we shall never forget. We shall always remember the debt we owe you – for we owe you everything. We owe you ourselves and our country.

Chapter 2

PLAYING ITS PART TO VICTORY: WOLVERHAMPTON

It was a fateful day, that Sunday 3 September when it seemed as if the whole nation was sat at a wireless, awaiting the words of Prime Minister Neville Chamberlain. A doom-laden stillness had fallen upon the land, as everyone prepared themselves to hear the worst. Just after eleven o'clock, Chamberlain's voice crackled across the air waves. He began by explaining that he was speaking from the Cabinet Room at 10 Downing Street and in burdened tones he went on to state, "This country is at war with Germany. You can imagine what a bitter blow it is to me that my long struggle to win peace has failed."

The declaration of war was inevitable. Two days previously, at 4:45 in the morning, fifty-eight German army divisions had invaded Poland, with which Britain had recently signed a mutual assistance treaty. The German leader had been warned that an invasion would lead to a British intervention but in his arrogance and lust for the domination of Europe, the Nazi dictator ignored that warning. Even then, as Polish troops valiantly defended their country, Chamberlain sought an opportunity to push back the clouds of war. On the night that Poland's integrity was violated, he addressed Parliament. He had few words to say, "for the time has come when action rather than speech is required. Eighteen months ago in this House I prayed that the responsibility might not fall upon me to ask this country to accept the awful arbitrament of war. I fear that I may not be able to avoid that responsibility."

Taking upon himself that unwanted yet unavoidable responsibility, Chamberlain said that with the support of France, the German Government had been told that unless they were prepared to give satisfactory assurances that they had had "suspended all aggressive action against Poland and are prepared promptly to withdraw their forces from Polish territory, His Majesty's Government in the United Kingdom will without hesitation fulfil their obligations to Poland."

The next day, Germany was given until 11.00 a.m. on 3 September to withdraw its troops from Poland. When that did not happen, the Prime Minister solemnly alerted the nation to the coming of war. The next day, the *Express and Star* asserted that the general attitude in Wolverhampton was, "Now we are in it, we must play our part in securing victory".

Like so many of his generation, Chamberlain's mind and soul had been seared by the terrible losses of life in the First World War. He had desperately wanted to avoid such a dreadful conflict again. As Prime Minister he had done all he could to keep peace in a Europe in which dictators destroyed their opponents and dowted the light of freedom. Just less than a year before, Chamberlain had returned from the Munich Conference with what he thought was an agreement with Hitler that in the future disputes between the United Kingdom and Germany would be settled by

Building Anderson Shelters in the back garden. Thanks to Wolverhampton Archives & Local Studies.

diplomacy. Arriving back at Heston Airport, Chamberlain had held up the paper upon which both leaders had signed and showed it to the crowds of people who had gathered. Confidently he declared that he had brought back, "Peace in our time".

Sadly, he had not. The ensuing aggression of Germany has led many to decry Chamberlain as an appeaser, as a weak leader who did not stand up to Hitler and who made Britain vulnerable to war. Others would argue that Chamberlain was not feeble, that his policy of trying to keep the peace was widely supported and that he actually bought time for Britain by his appeasement, valuable time in which Britain rearmed.

Certainly, preparations for war had begun in earnest some years before. As early as 1935, procedures had been put in place for training experts who would co-ordinate civilian responses if war broke out and there were air raids on Britain's great towns and cities. Leaflets were also sent out about Air Raid Precautions (ARP) and in 1937 Wolverhampton Council, amongst others, established an Air Raid Precautions (ARP) Committee. It divided the borough into fifteen districts and appointed 258 street wardens. Two years later, nearby Tettenhall Urban District Council joined other local authorities in producing a booklet telling people what to do after an air raid.

By this time, public air raid shelters had started to appear locally as had shadow factories – like that put up by H. M. Hobson at Fordhouses in Wolverhampton. This site had been bought in 1939 and building soon started on a works of almost 25,000 square feet. It was camouflaged to blend in with the countryside, whilst a total blackout meant that artificial light had to be used morning and night. Air raid shelters were erected on the south side of the factory and in June 1940 the place was ready to commence operations.

Founded in 1911, H. M. Hobson specialised in the design and manufacture of carburettors and automatic controls for aero engines. Under the foremanship of Mr J. Cotterill, twelve workers began machining raw castings to make aluminium carburettor bodies for fighter and bomber aircraft engines, such as the Cheetah Engines which powered the Avro Anson. Slowly the workforce increased, and when they were not at their jobs they acted as voluntary fire wardens to protect the plant from an incendiary attack.

The carburettors made at Fordhouses were vital and the workers grafted seven days a week to turn out as many as they could. By 1941, over 50 people were engaged in production, the premises were protected by the Home Guard, and another shadow factory had been built by the Ministry of Aircraft Production just to the north. This No. 2 Works was headed by Harold Price, who oversaw milling and drilling operations on the carburettor bodies for the No. 1 Works. The next year, the size of the works was more than doubled and work began on the BH5, a bulk fuel injection system for the Hercules Engine.

Fordhouses was becoming a vital element in the munitions industry and by 1945 the development of a Fitting Shop and Petrol Test had allowed the total manufacture of carburettors on site. There were few British aircraft not supplied by Hobson's and when they took to the skies, pilots of planes such as the Blenheim, Halifax, Lancaster, Spitfire, Tempest and Wellington all relied on the skills of Wolverhampton workers.

Other local factories played as important a role in the fight against tyranny, amongst them Boulton Paul Aircraft Ltd. A Norwich company, its aircraft division had relocated to Wolverhampton in 1936 to expand the business and to take advantage of the skilled labour force in the area. It was also believed that if war were to come that the new factory would be in an area safer from enemy bombing than in East Anglia. During the war Boulton Paul produced at its Pendeford site 2,198 aircraft, including the Defiant, a two-seater fighter which despite its later reputation did have success initially.

The design work on the Defiant itself had begun back in Norwich three years before war was declared. In place of a fixed-firing armament it had a multi-gun turret. The employment of a gunner reduced the workload for the pilot, whilst the armaments in the turret allowed a greater field of fire. The Defiant entered service in May 1940 and did well, but the Germans pilots learned that the Defiant was less agile than their own fighter planes and so attacked the Defiant head on or from below, where its guns could not be trained. Consequently the Defiant was fitted as a night fighter and then for target-towing duties.

*22nd Battalion South Staffs Home Guard. Thanks to Wolverhampton Archives &
Local Studies.*

From 1942, Boulton Paul also made the Barracuda, and gun-turrets for aircraft. The
Germans were aware of the importance of this aircraft factory and Luftwaffe maps
from 1940 show it clearly. To fool enemy aircraft, a 'dummy' factory with 'dummy'
aircraft outside was built two miles away at Coven. It did its job for it was bombed three
times. In common with Fordhouses, Boulton Paul had a unit of the Home Guard. They
were not on their own. The factories of Joseph Sankey and Stewart's and Lloyds in
Bilston were under the watch of the 34th Company, as were other industrial premises.

Guy Motors Ltd was another important centre of war work. Back in 1923 it had
commenced production of military vehicles, and five years later it was making a six-
wheeled armoured car for the Indian Government. In the late 1930s Guy's was heavily
involved in the production of lorries and gun tractors for the British Army, and
produced the first British rear-engined, four-wheeled drive, all-welded Armoured Car.

These were considered of such high quality and safety that they were used for
the protection of the Royal Family and the Prime Minister, Winston Churchill,
during the war. Indeed, the company's development of armoured plate welding in

place of riveting was believed to have saved the country one hundred million pounds in tank production costs. As in many other factories, women workers made a significant impact at Guy's, with the firm employing over two hundred women full time and more than three hundred part time.

One of them was Mrs Nicklin. She had eleven children, eight of whom were still living, and worked fifty-five hours a week at the Guy Motors factory. Described as a five foot high and seven stone, forty-three year old Mrs Nicklin still found the time to cook, wash, clean and mend for her family on Sundays. She also returned home during her lunch break each day to "tidy and clean up and get food ready for cooking a dinner at night". Fittingly she was described by the *Express and Star* as Wolverhampton's hardest worker!

Women were as prominent at Villiers, working on machines, assembly and production – indeed in the engine assembly shop sixty percent of the workers were female. In the First World War, this concern had produced ammunition, in particular fuses for the Vickers 75mm shell, and during the Second World War it manufactured fuses for anti-aircraft, artillery and cannon shells, as well as motorcycle engines and cycle parts for use by the armed forces. By the end of the war Villiers could boast that it had made in excess of 6 million shell fuses, 5 million fuses for cannon shells, 17 million steel forgings, 750,000 bomb parts, 14,000 magnetos and thousands of cycle parts.

Goodyear's contribution to victory was equally impressive. Having set up in Wolverhampton in the 1920s, Goodyear switched to war production in 1939. Its employees worked as hard as anyone, with twenty days on and one day off. A fine

Women workers at Guy's. Thanks to Wolverhampton Archives & Local Studies.

War work at Boulton Paul.

example was set by Walter Hazlett, the managing director, who travelled to work by bus and also drove an ambulance two nights a week. Protected by its own Home Guard detachment, Goodyear quickly became the second largest producer of aircraft tyres in Britain, making tyres as big as five feet in height, 24 inches wide and weighing some 355 pounds.

Then in 1942 it was faced with a major challenge. With Britain now at war with Japan, 90%of its supplies of raw materials were in the hands of the enemy.

Acting with initiative, the company looked for other work and began making plywood panels for pontoon bridges. As was reported in the *Express and Star* on 14 March 1945, they were "impregnated with water-proof glue and cured under pressure. 14,000 of these panels were made." In the spring of 1943, synthetic rubber began to arrive from the Unites States. This allowed the release of some of the reserve stocks of natural rubber and output quickly rose. The company also produced rubber hoses for pumping water, petrol and oil, and a self-buoyant armoured hose for use in the refuelling of ships.

The *Express and Star* highlighted yet another ingenious Wolverhampton firm. On 6 April 1945 it brought to the fore one of the most successful production innovations of the war. This was "the policy of dispersal by handing out the work of producing many small components to small concerns, such as peace-time garages converted for the purpose". This initiative came about after Dunkirk "to meet the vitally urgent need for producing armaments for defence, and amongst the first to see how important it would be was Industrial Designs Ltd, a Wolverhampton firm whose function is what the name suggests – they undertake the planning, layout, jigging and tooling of industrial plant for all purposes".

As the *Express and Star* reporter emphasised, many back-yard manufacturers "were put on their feet in those early days and directed along the path to steady production. To many the firm's experts have returned since to replan and increase

The Mayor of Wolverhampton, Councillor T. W. Phillipson, with the town clerk, Mr J. Brock Allon, leading the procession of aldermen and councillors to the civic service of thanksgiving at Darlington Street Church, Wolverhampton on the evening of VE Day.

output capacity." At the same time, Industrial Designs Ltd had been called in to advise and help the Ministry of Aircraft Production "and for 12 months a team of experts was engaged on jigging and tooling a Ministry underground factory". Its expertise had also been essential in transforming two Scottish factories, the one making carpets and the other linoleum, into centres for the production of torpedoes.

It was declared that there was hardly a section of the war industry untouched by the small but highly skilled team at Industrial Designs Ltd and it was estimated that the company had handled some 35,000 designs during the war and been involved at many top secret establishments in inaccessible locations. Many of the jigs and tools needed by the Wolverhampton business were produced by Dellmich Engineering, based in the same premises – a former mission hall.

One more inventive company was Star Aluminium. By 1942 this was making 2,500 miles of aluminium foil each week, large amounts of which were dropped over Germany to fox radar operators. And at the Beacon Works of John Thompson Motor Pressings, chassis frames for military vehicles as well as twenty-five pounder gun trailers were manufactured. On top of that, the firm's workers supplied two-pounder anti-tank shields, anti-aircraft gun elevating gear, and pontoons. That was not the sum of the company's achievements, for it also made Rotol airscrews for Spitfires and Hurricanes, tank ribs for Blenheim bombers, rudder arm masts for Wellington bombers, gun covers for Gloster Gladiators, seats for air gunners and much more.

Given its wide-ranging involvement in the munitions industry, Wolverhampton was an obvious target for German bombers. A German bombing map from 1939 marked out Guy's, Ever Ready Ltd, the gas works, railway workshops and Electrical Construction Ltd. The Luftwaffe had similar maps for Bilston and Wednesfield, whilst it had access to lists of industries and airfields locally. It also knew that Wolverhampton was defended by 'Flakbaterie' using 9.4 cm shells.

In late November 1940 a decoded message indicated that Wolverhampton was to be attacked with Coventry and Birmingham. After the devastating raids on the two Warwickshire cities, in which hundreds of people were killed, extra anti-aircraft guns were sent to Wolverhampton. These were spotted by German aerial reconnaissance and as a result the town was spared from bombing. However, there were raids in October 1940, August 1942 and at the end of July 1942 when incendiaries were dropped for four nights in a row over a wide area. Sadly eight people were killed, whilst much damage was caused to homes and public buildings. At the Royal Hospital staff in the ARP (Air Raid Precautions) kicked fire bombs off the roof, whilst down below air raid wardens gathered them up and made them ineffective.

Thankfully, the tide of war had now begun to turn and at last in May 1945 Germany capitulated. The people of Wolverhampton could proudly assert that they kept their word. Just as they had said they would do in September 1939, they had played their part in bringing about victory.

Chapter 3

SOLDIER FRED'S PRECIOUS
RECORD OF FIGHT IN FRANCE

Barrie Blower of Walsall kindly sent me some papers left behind by the late Fred Boot, a friend of Barrie's deceased mother-in-law, Ethel Machin. Hailing from Gower Street on The Pleck in Walsall, Fred was a sergeant who wrote a diary of his experiences of the D. Day landings in Normandy. He also carried with him a poem, which Barrie has thoughtfully transposed for me as the paper that it is written on is badly stained.

Barrie affirms that "it is essential to keep in touch with the past as our history is what the future is built on." Barrie is right and I thank him for sending me this extraordinary, moving and thought-provoking document. I should like to pay tribute to Barrie and all the work that he has done for the well-being of working people in Walsall and indeed the West Midlands as a whole. He has given his time tirelessly and freely and is respected by myself and so many others for his determination to make our region a better place in which all of us can live with respect.

Fred Boot's compelling account of the D Day landings is an invaluable historical source. We have many accounts of the D Day landings written years after the events, but this is the first description that I have come across written at the time by a foot soldier. I defy anybody not to be moved by Fred's account and by his poem, filled as they are with Christian faith and sympathy for his enemies as much as for his pals. Fred must have been a wonderful man and must have been imbued with his positive values in his upbringing on The Pleck.

I have tried to follow Fred's movements during the Battle for Normandy and place them within the broader context of the military operations. The D Day landings on 6 June 1944 were part of Operation Overlord, the codename for the Allied invasion of north-west Europe; whilst Operation Neptune was the assault phase of this invasion - which involved landing the troops on the beaches and all the supporting operations required to establish a beachhead in France. Operation Neptune began on D-Day (6 June 1944) and ended on 30 June 1944.

Fred mentions HMS 'Rodney'. This was one of six battleships which bombarded the enemy positions and it was responsible for attacking the enemy positions around 'Sword' Beach. It would seem then, that Fred landed at Sword, although he also mentions HMS 'Black Prince' which was aiming its guns at German positions around 'Utah' Beach, where the Americans landed. Landings began on 'Sword' Beach at 7.25 in the morning, following a successful attack inland by the 6th Airborne Division at Ranville. The beach itself had been marked out by crews of midget submarines, whilst the troops that came ashore were part of the British Third Infantry Division.

This division had taken part in the retreat to Dunkirk back in 1940 - a retreat to which Fred alludes in his poem. Fred points out that he and his mates had to clamber down scrub netting from their ship to the landing craft and that it was a rough sea. Indeed it was. A gale in The English Channel and a strong westerly wind had whipped up the water so that the sea ran high on to the beach itself. There was stiff resistance from the German 716th Infantry Division, but

Fred Boot in uniform.

supported by DD tanks, the British forces made ground. It was on Sword Beach that occurred the famous scene of Bill Millin, the piper of Lord Lovatt's Commandoes, playing his pipes to raise the spirits of the British.

Led by Major General Rennie, DSO, MBE, the British were charged with taking Caen, nine miles inland, and linking up with the 6th Airborne across the River Orne at Ranville. The taking of Caen did not go to plan, but the British attack drew in so many German troops and tanks that it took pressure off the Americans to the west.

Fred notes that on the first night he and his unit made it to Creully. Interestingly this was taken by troops belonging to the 3rd Canadian Division, made up of Canadian and British men, which had landed at 'Juno' Beach. The Battle for Caen was as fierce as Fred relates and lasted for weeks, until the town was taken on 7 July.

The General Von Kluge mentioned by Fred took over as German High Commander five days previously. He committed suicide on 18 August, following the failed attempt to assassinate Hitler by German Army Officers. By this date the Allied breakthrough from Normandy had been achieved. Men like Fred Boot were vital in the crucial Battle for Normandy which was so vital in the liberation of France and the defeat of the Nazis.

Fred Boot. The D. Day Landings Normandy 1944

May 1944

We are now stationed in Hull. Every day we go to Bridlington and practice running up the cliffs in full marching order. We realize that we are practising for a forthcoming invasion of France. We move down south to Horsham under canvass, and take all our vehicles to be waterproofed and have the exhaust pipes brought up the sides of the vehicles. All the lorry cabs have gun turrets fitted, so we have no illusions that it is nearly time to go. We practise driving through water in the local village pond. Most of us get stuck, as the water reaches our tummies, causing our feet to come off the pedals.

June 1944

The company is divided into three sections. We of number one section are separated from the others in the camp, and are told that we are leaving for an unknown destination. I try to see my friend Bill Brabbins but am not allowed.

We leave Horsham, and are told that we are off to Tilbury. I wonder what we are going into, but comfort myself that nothing could be worse than the flying bombs that are dropping at various intervals around the area all then while. We are fitted out, (Mae Wests) and sick bags, and then board a troop ship at the West Indies docks. We are put to sea, but have to return when fire breaks out in the hold, they say it is through spontaneous combustion. We are delayed for three hours, we eventually stop off at Southend to pick up the rest of our convoy. I am aboard the EMPIRE TAVENER which is the flag ship of the convoy and carries the commodore. We take turns mine watching and can see the muzzle blasts from the German guns firing from Calais. We then transfer to a landing craft having to clamber down scrub netting in a rough sea to the craft which was a job in itself, wearing full marching order. We get to the shore, and wade through a foot of water. The shells from the 'Rodney' and 'Black Prince' are thundering over our heads and the first German aircraft comes across firing cannons.

Equipment of every kind strewn about interspersed with dead bodies. As night approaches we are relived that we are still in one piece and able to deal

British and Canadian troops wading to the beach at Besnieres, Normandy. They are carrying bicycles and are struggling through the high tide on 6 June 1944.

with the task of digging in. We try to get some fitful rest but that is impossible owing to enemy aircraft and shells. We move up at night to Creully and once more dig ourselves in. As soon as the dusk falls the sky is alive with flying Bofor shells. They are shelling an airstrip about three miles away. The sensation is terrible, as the sound is deafening when they are coming nearer. Three Boche aircraft dive down, and I see the bombs released from their plane. Luckily we are spared but feeling a little shellshocked. Almost immediately six Spitfires are up. One of the Jerries goes down in flames, whilst one of the others shoots away. I can not help but admire the last one who fights it out to the last. We see smoke falling from its tail and are glad when we see his parachute open. Such as this occurs several times each day. It is very queer to see our bombers passing over at night on their way to bomb Germany, when underneath the Jerries are bombing us. We move up to Brettsville with the Fifteenth Scottish Infantry and sad to say, lose our first man. Len Greenman is killed when a Jerry mortar explodes a yard away from him. A feeling of depression comes over me as you can not help but wonder who will be next.

At about 7 o'clock we are told to be ready to move, as Jerry has broken through with 15 Tiger tanks. We fall back dragging our camouflage netting still over our vehicles. A Fifteenth Scottish puts one of the tanks out with a PIAT which has

A group of wounded Canadian soldiers waiting to be taken to a Casualty Clearing Station on 7 June 1944.

pierced three inches of steel. The charred bodies of the crew are sprawled about inside. We move up to Brettsville-En-Bassin just outside Caen. We are told to dig in because of the offensive to take Caen which is starting. I see the first thousand bomber raid. The sky is black with 'Lancasters' and 'Halifaxes'. They all circle the target and go in and out dropping their bombs despite the German Ack Ack being thrown up at them in Golden Torrents. We have to lie in our dug outs because of the blasts which seem to make the ground jump up and down. I am sorry to see four of our planes slowly shrivel to the ground in flames. The artillery opens up incessantly with 7.2 and 5.5 for six hours. Surely nothing can be left alive.

Now at last we attack, but instead of Jerry being wiped out they have appeared out of cellars and underground fortifications and completely surprised our infantry. We bring our wounded to the advanced dressing station which is just behind us. Twenty ambulances alone, carry six hundred wounded during the day. It is impossible to describe the terrible wounds that some of our lads have got. HOW CAN THE HUMAN RACE INFLICT SUCH A WASTE OF LIFE ON EACH OTHER?

Fresh batches of infantry move along to the front whistling as they march, many of them for the last time. At last Caen is taken. At the edge of the roadside, even in

British assault troops and Red Cross personnel landing on a beach in Normandy on 7 June.

the middle of the crossroads the pathetic little army-issue white crosses, are scattered about those killed in action. We have been at the front unrelieved, three weeks and have now been sent back for a rest to Creully which is now about seven miles behind the line. While we are, the offensive fore the crossing of the river starts, and we are grieved to see the ambulance blown up with Bert Danks and Hank driving. It was got when the road was shelled as we were trying to cross a small bridge. All that was left were fragments of clothing and bits of flesh splattered over the cab. Only by seeing such as this, can anyone realise what war really is.

We cross the river and go to Douvres and lose two vehicles, when Jerry dive bombs the convoy which luckily is parked away from our dugout. Everywhere, Jerry dead are lying about black as charcoal, and stinking like hell. We move to St Jean des Esartiers and lose our Fifth lad. Harry Freesnan is shot through lung, and dies a short while after. We stay the night in a French Chateau which had been the home of the Bishop of Calvoudos. It had been occupied a few hours before. Half eaten meals of black bread and potatoes were left by the Jerries. We found a 30 gallon keg of Calvados and have a night of forgetfulness on the strength of it.

So, on to Bausnont or what is left of it after being bombed by our planes and then shelled to the ground. All around, dozens of dead cows bloated, twice their size are lying about. We get a two hour attack of vomiting, as the stench is indescribable. Already hundreds of German troops are giving themselves up. How dejected they look. Dozens of our lads are killed when the tanks keep continually bombing our lines, and our lads are mad!

The fifteenth Scottish lose hundreds of men when they are caught in a creeping barrage from our own artillery. We have been unable to fetch our clothes off for 4 weeks, but have to when I am soaked to the skin after sleeping in the drenching rain with only a ground sheet for cover. How little those people back home realise the meaning of war!

We get our first big meal when we have to shoot a cow that is badly wounded in the leg and side. We cross the line and are engaged in the greatest battle in Mornsville. General Von Kluge is in command of the German seventh army which is now surrounded, and hounded from land and air. A great victory is achieved leaving thousands dead and wounded. Literally thousands of vehicles and tanks are scattered everywhere, and also we learn that up to two thousand horses were killed. JUST INNOCENT VICTIMS OF MAN'S INHUMANITY TO MAN.

Poem (carried by Fred Boot, Pleck, Walsall)

Stay with me God the night is dark
The night is cold and my little spark
of courage dims, the night is long
Be with me God and make me strong.

I love a game, I love a fight
I hate the dark, I love the light.
I love my child, I love my wife
I am no coward but I do love life.

Life with its change of mood
And shade, I want to live
I'm not afraid, but me and mine are hard to part
O unknown God lift up my heart.

You stilled the waters at Dunkirk
And saved your servants, all your work
So wonderful, dear God you strode
Before us down the dreadful road.

We were alone all hope had fled
We loved our country and our dead
And could not shame them so we stayed
The course, and tried not to be afraid.

Dear God that nightmare road and the sea
When we got there we
Were men, my eyes were blind, my feet were torn
But my soul sang like a bird at dawn.

I know that death is but a door
I know what we are fighting for
Peace for our kids, our brothers freed
A kinder world, a better creed.

I'm but the man my brother bore
A simple man and nothing more
But God of strength and gentleness
Be pleased to make me nothing less.

Help me again when the dark is near
To mock the haggard face of fear
So when I fall, if fall I must
My soul triumph in the dust

Mary Gittings was moved by the account of the D Day experiences of Sergeant Fred Boot and informed me that this poem was not written by him. She explains that "I think it is likely to have been found by him and copied out to keep in his wallet or packet – as many soldiers did with meaningful writings at that time. I found the poem in an anthology called 'A Book of Comfort', edited by Elizabeth Goudge, printed by Collins in 1964, the note saying that it was first published anonymously but the author is stated as Gerald Kersh, who was, I believe a professional writer."

Following on from the article about Fred Boot of The Pleck in Walsall and his first-hand account of the D Day landings, Robert James Boot of Great Wyrley dropped me a letter to tell me that "Fred was my father's nephew and known to my two brothers and myself as Uncle Fred. Fred was born in Walsall and lived in Beacon Street in The Chuckery in his early years in the same house as my father. They moved to The Pleck where he and his parents lived in Gower Street all their lives. Fred left school to work with his father, an apprentice coppersmith and tinsmith, where he went on to be very skilled in his trade.

A VE Day Party on The Pleck, where Fred grew up and lived for many years.

"Fred was called up into the Army in the early part of the war and served for six years in the RASC as a field ambulance driver, mostly in North Africa and Europe. He was attached to the 15th Scottish Division in Normandy. When he was serving in Holland, during the fighting he came across a young girl five or six years old separated from her family, wandering about in all the shooting and fighting. He picked her up and after a time managed to get her to the Red Cross station. He left the young girl with them and somehow they managed to unite her with her family. Many years after the war this young girl, who was now grown up and married with children, tracked Fred down through the Army. She invited Fred to see her again. Fred went and after that used to go to Holland to see her often.

"When Fred left the Army he decided to work for himself repairing car bodywork. He did this for the rest of his working life at his garage up the road in Gower Street. Fred became well known and sought after for his skill with metal. People have told me, and I have seen it for myself, that Fred could work metal like no-one else, although Fred always said he was nowhere near as good as his Dad.

"Fred married but unfortunately lost his wife Doris in the sixties. Fred was an animal lover and always had a dog, his beloved Borzois (Russian wolf hounds). He used to walk them in Pleck Park where he and the dogs were almost a landmark.

Being an animal lover he never turned away sick and injured waifs and strays brought to him from people all over The Pleck.

"You were right when you said about his upbringing in The Pleck. He loved his mother and father and said what good parents they were to him and his sisters Gwen and Doreen. Gwen lived round the corner from Fred and looked after him like a mother for 30 years after his wife died. When Gwen died in 1997, this was a turning point in Fred's life, and within two years Fred unfortunately died from cancer at the age of 78.

"Fred loved poetry and reading and was largely self taught. One of his favourite poems was 'Blue Remembered Hills' by A. E. Housman. Fred also liked his sport, cricket in particular. He also loved his gardening. Roses were his favourite. Fred made regular trips to Europe as a member of the Normandy Veterans, Market Gardens Veterans and the 8th Army Veterans."

Fred later in life paying his respects to fallen comrades at a memorial in France.

Chapter 4

BLACK COUNTRY STALWARTS

Escape from the Germans: John Perry

Ann Macefield of Barncroft Road, Tividale has a great pride in her father – and when you read the account of his bravery and daring you will also share that pride. John Thomas William Perry was born in Tipton and was a relation of Bill Perry, the Tipton Slasher. John must have inherited the bravery and fortitude of his famed relation, because in the Second World War he escaped from his Prisoner of War Camp and managed to evade capture and reach the safety of Turkey, which was a neutral country at the time.

John's wife, Agnes Irene Perry died in 1998, but importantly during the war she had written down an account of John's escape. It is a remarkable and rare piece of evidence and Pauline has sent it to me not only in honour of her Dad but also in honour of her Mom's love for him. A motor mechanic from Horseley Heath, John became a gunner in the Royal Artillery when he joined up. Sent to Greece, he and his pals were ordered to keep a front line clear but soon were surrounded by German paratroopers. The British lads fought on until only nine were left alive "when the arrival of additional German troops forced them to surrender. The parachutists who captured them did not treat them at all badly but this could not be said of the guards at the Salonika Prison Camp to which they were taken.

"There was lots of work but little to eat. The prisoners had to work from 6 a.m. to 6 p.m. and would have starved had it not been for the kindly Greeks who brought them as much food as they could. Bombardier Perry is full of praise for the Greeks. They are brave no doubt, still doing all they can. The Greek people hope that the day is not far off when British soldiers will again be on their soil. Greece is still a malaria infested country and many of the German troops have suffered from this disease. Fortunately Bombardier Perry contracted malaria otherwise he would not have been taken to hospital and would never have been able to escape.

"The German military hospital had no room for prisoners and he was taken to a Greek hospital where nurses and doctors did their best for him. Civilian clothes were smuggled into the building and on one pretext or another he was kept in hospital longer than was necessary. One night he and a Greek officer hid, dressed in civilian clothes and with the assistance of some of the nurses was able to elude the guards and escape.

"Through the good offices of an American a car was procured which took them to the coast where a motor boat was found which took them to Mytilene. They had to hide in a little place for two days, where a small sailing boat ferried them to Turkey and safety. The Turks did not send a brass band to meet them, they were instead locked up in a quarantine station. The British Consul however was notified and after ten days arrangements were made for them to proceed to Egypt.

"They travelled by train which passed through Ankara, the new Turkish capital, a very impressive place. In Cairo it was again found necessary to take him to hospital from where he was later to evacuate to South Africa. He is now a patient in Oribii and is rapidly recovering health and strength. He hopes the day is not far distant when he will be able to fight again."

Amazingly, when he was in Cairo, John was able to send greetings to his wife via the wireless, as was recorded in the *Express and Star*. Agnes was then living in 3 court, 1 house, Providence Street, Great Bridge. John's message to her began with him saying "Hello Agnes, this is Jack speaking". He told her that he was in one piece was still smiling and asked her to tell his father about the message. John finished off by sending Agnes his love and stating. "Don't worry about me. They are looking after me very well here."

Reading the matter of fact way in which Agnes wrote down John's audacious escape and harking at the down to earth manner in which he assured her that he was fine, you can feel and hear the strength of character of Englishmen and women such as these who fought and worked for our freedom. As Saint George's Day approaches, let us wear our red roses with respect in memory of men and women such as John and Agnes Perry - Tiptonians, Black Country folk and proud English people prepared to give their lives for liberty, tolerance and democracy.

John Thomas William Perry.

Proud Black Country Mon: Jack Stokes

The Black Country has recently lost one its stalwarts, Jack Stokes of Wednesbury. I met Jack a good few years back when I was invited to pop over to Wednesbury and talk with the Old Newtowners, a smashing group of people keeping alive the memories of both their town and their neighbourhood. In the ensuing years, I met

Jack on a number of occasions, most recently when I gave a talk at Saint Bartholomew's, the parish church of Wednesbury high up on the hill. Each time I spoke with Jack, I recognised that I was in the company of a man who was imbued with the spirit of the Black Country – hard-collaring, dogged, resolute, unyielding to wrongdoing, caring for the needs of others and proud.

For me, Jack Stokes was the epitome of a Black Country chap. Like so many, he may not have had great wealth but yet he gave so much back and that which he gave back was worth more than money and property, for Jack gave of himself. He was dedicated to doing all he that could to improve life for the people of Wednesbury and he was committed to working on behalf of the folk to whom he belonged – the working class of the Black Country. I am privileged to have met Jack and known him; I am honoured that he shared his stories with me; and I am proud to have spoken with a man whose words and deeds drew me into the lore and ways of the Black Country.

I saw in Jack the same grit and guts of my own Nan and Grandad. There were so many like them and we are losing them so fast. With their passing goes the world forged by our forebears, a world in which we grew up and a world which is being swept away so quickly. But thanks to Jack and those like him, we shall never forget that which we owe to him and his kind – our very being. Rest in peace, Jack. You did your work and you did it well. We shall not forget your or your people, for you made us.

Trevor, Jack's son, tells me that his Dad was born on 12 February 1922 in Great Western Street, Wednesbury. Jack's father worked on the railways for the LMS, but at the age of five Jack was orphaned and went to live with a family named Spittle who resided in Crankhall Lane, Wednesbury. From here, he attended Mesty Croft Infants and Juniors School and then went on to Holyhead Road Secondary School, Wednesbury. After leaving school, Jack

Jack Stokes in uniform with a friend he made out in Sydney and after whom he named his son, Trevor.

took up painting and decorating, and on the outbreak of the Second World War he took a job in a reserved occupation at the Old Park Works, Wednesbury, building tanks for the war effort. In 1942 he volunteered for service in the Royal Navy and he was attached to the DEM's, Defensively Equipped Merchant Ships, serving mainly out of Australia.

In 1945 Jack married Evelyn Burrows at Wednesbury Registrar Office and after the war he worked in local industry. He has two sons and two grandchildren. Jack was first elected to Wednesbury Borough Council in the mid 1950s and served the people of his beloved town until the borough was dissolved in 1966. He then went on to serve on the newly created authority of West Bromwich and afterwards on Sandwell Council, until he retired from public life. It was whilst he was on the West Bromwich Council that Jack became Deputy Mayor of the town.

Jack and Evelyn Stokes two days after their marriage.

Jack was an ardent supporter of West Bromwich Albion, having being a fan from 1927 and having watching his first game in the early 1930s. His other pastime was the Old Newtowners at Mesty Croft, a group which he helped to form for former pupils from the 1920s and 1930s. Until two years ago he was also a very active member on the Royal British Legion. Jack passed away on the 20th April 2004 just before midnight. Trevor adds that "I do have to put this as a foot note, and he'll be laughing about this in heaven, and it's that Dad was born a proud Black Country Mon, but he died a Brummie as he was in the Queen Elizabeth!"

From Burma to the Manor

Robert Farmer contacted me regarding his father, Alfred T. Farmer - best known as Jim Farmer. Jim asked Robert to write to me "with a story he produced for an internal publication produced on the 50th anniversary of the NHS. He thought that it may be of some interest to your readers. My Father is now coming up to 82 and still works three mornings a week on accident and emergency at the Manor assisting the admin staff and being a friend to all those who walk into the place.

"He is a 'people person' and thrives on his uncanny ability to talk to everyone and anyone putting them at their ease in what is often a stressful situation. He lost his wife Win, some five years ago now after nursing her through six years of cancer and his caring role carries on even now. Dad has many such stories to tell, especially from around the Second World War, but he thought some of the things mentioned about the Manor in particular may kindle some memories for others."

Here is Jim's story:

My journey to the Manor Hospital began from a bamboo operating table two hundred and fifty miles inside Japanese lines in Burma during 1944. As Private Farmer I was attached to a deep penetration force known as the Chindits, commanded by General Wingate; our job was to destroy all Japanese communications stooping them from getting into India. During this campaign we destroyed railroads, ammunition dumps and mine roads. Conditions were appalling – snakes, leeches and tics were common place coupled with no sanitation, drinking water came from rivers purified with tablets; a good guide were our mules, they would not go anywhere near poisoned water. The mules were also our transport, and we were supplied with food and medical items by parachute drops.

Four mouths after arriving in Burma the monsoons started, this meant that we were soaking wet morning and night, after five months inside enemy lines we marched to a place called Mogaug. Here was a railway siding that was held by the Japanese, it was our job to attack and capture the site. We decided to go early in the morning but after have formed up to take it we found that the Japanese were too strong for us. On going back to the position we came from a Japanese machine gun opened fire and I caught one of the bullets, it penetrated my chest cavity, passed right through me and came out of my back. The sensation of being shot was a hot feeling – not pain at first and I remained conscious throughout.

My mate George Cartwright who was with my took one of his puttees off and tied it round me. He got me out of the trench and through all the bullets and shells that were falling and carried me on his back to the dressing station. How he found the strength to do this I will never know, we were all seven stone weaklings after months in the jungle without proper food. There a medical orderly gave me an injection for the pain, they put me on a bamboo stretcher and four

Jim as a teenager standing with his father, Alfred Thomas Farmer.

Burmese civilians carried me shoulder high for two hours to a safer place. The medical officer – a Captain, told them to put me on a bamboo table under a nearby tree, he took out a dagger from his puttee and slit my shirt off, then he said "start counting" as he gave me an injection, I can still remember reaching twelve.

Next morning I came round and I was on a stretcher in a bamboo hut, I was desperate for a drink and to relieve myself, they came and told me that within the hour I would be flown out on light plane holding only two people. We were flown to a larger airstrip where I transferred to a Dakota and was taken to a military hospital in Assam. From here on I took in five different hospitals finally being transferred from Glasgow on my journey back to the Manor Hospital in Walsall, my hometown.

Jim in his Bush hat just prior to going into Burma in the Second World War.

Jim (left) and his mate George Cartwright (now deceased).

There were two soldier wards at the Manor; I reported to the officer in charge and he put me onto ward four. The ward was completely open, no cubicles or curtains, all beds pushed up against the walls. Most noticeable were two coal burning stoves in the middle of the ward, one at the foot of my bed; it always puzzled me where the smoke went. I turned out that there was a flue coming out of the back of the stoves that went into the floor, and when they lit the stoves in winter the ward filled with smoke. At the base of my bed was a little trap door in the floor, they opened it up and pushed some newspaper inside and lit it with a match. This drew the smoke from the stoves out into chimneys outside which still exist to this day.

I found that it was a strict place but the staff was very friendly especially to the wounded soldiers, however everyone including nurses and patients were referred to by their rank and surname only. There was a Matron in charge and her word was law, unfortunately her name escapes me but I can remember Sister Lockley, Nurse Rose, Nurse Evens and Nurse Price. Breakfast was at 7.30am, then all the beds were drawn into the middle of the ward and wet tea leaves from the morning brew were thrown onto the floor to settle any dust, the nurses would then sweep this up. The beds were then pushed back and the floor polished, this happened every day except Sundays.

Everyone had to go back to bed after breakfast, the beds were made with box pleats, a quilt was on the bottom of each bed and this was pulled up for the daily visit of the Doctor, Matron or Sister. As soon as they were gone the beds were turned back again and we were allowed to get up and sit around the stoves.

All soldiers had to wear Hospital Blue, on occasions we were allowed to go down to the town; you had to have permission from the Sister and you had to be back by 8pm. One or two nights we were late getting back, we had been for a drink in the Four Cups in Park Street. We would get back into the

Finally in the late 1980s Jim sent for his medals, unfortunately George Cartwright, his mate who helped him in the jungle had passed away, but Dad invited George's son to present him with his medals at the family's church, St John' Walsall Wood.

hospital up the fire escape, Matron got wind of this and next time we did it a figure appeared at the top and there stood Matron in the middle of the doorway, arms folded – we pushed past her very sheepishly, not a word was spoken and we never did it again.

My real reason for still being in hospital was for the constant bouts of Malaria I suffered as a result of mosquito bites in Burma. The treatment consisted of stone hot water bottles down the sides and along the bottom of the bed, quinine and other tablets; I was even rushed back in on one Boxing Day.

Most of the other patients were from the second front; they arrived after midnight on the Red Cross trains. If it were light or early evening they would be shunted into sidings until it was dark so that seeing them would not damage public morale. I can remember going to sleep one night in the ward where I was completely alone and when I awoke the ward was full. From the Manor I was taken to the Tropical Fever Hospital in Burntwood where my malaria was finally cleared up and I was discharged.

Now, sixty years on I have made it back to the Manor again and have been a WRVS volunteer in the Accident and Emergency department since the new part of the hospital opened a number of years ago now and I can say with some conviction that things have certainly changed.

Chapter 5

WOLF GUARDS, HUGUENOTS AND GLASS MAKING: WORDSLEY

For generations untold wolves have figured, some would say unjustly, as animals to be feared, hated and hunted. Portrayed as evil, savage and cunning, wolves have spawned one of the most frightening creatures of mythology - the werewolf, a man who is transformed into a bloodthirsty wolf. Still for all that wolves were loathed as killers of sheep and as intelligent animals unafraid of people, they did have a mystique upon them that attracted as much as it repelled humans.

Adaptable and hardy, wolves were able to survive in the most inhospitable fastnesses, but even here they were chased to the death. From the time that they conquered England in 1066, the Norman kings made use of wolf hunters, who were granted land if they were successful, and the numbers of wolves declined drastically. Then in 1281, Edward I – the Hammer of the Scots who also overwhelmed the last independent Welsh kingdom - ordered the extermination of all wolves in England. He employed a Peter Corbet, perhaps a member of the powerful Shropshire family of that name, to "take and destroy all the wolves he could find" in Gloucestershire, Herefordshire, Worcestershire, Shropshire and Staffordshire".

It seems that Edward's campaign was mostly successful, although wolves may have survived for a century or more in the most remote spots in the realm. Certainly, by the end of the fifteenth century there was no doubt – wolves were extinct in England. But if they themselves had been destroyed their presence lingers on in artefacts, personal names and place names from the Anglo-Saxon period.

During this time the wolf was associated with one of the leading royal families – that of the Wuffingas, the people of the wolf. Rulers of the kingdom of East Anglia from the late 500s, the importance of wolves to this dynasty was revealed in the burial ship excavated at Sutton Hoo. Dating from about 625, amongst the jewellery, coins and weapons found in this magnificent treasure trove were the frame and mounts of a purse lid. Made of gold with decorations in gold filigree, cut garnet (red) and millefiori glass in blue, red and white, it is a superb work of art that shows prominently the figures of two men. Each of them is flanked by upstanding wolves with their mouths open.

It is impossible to ascertain how common wolves were in Anglo-Saxon England, although many male names include the word wolf. Amongst them were Wulfhere, a king of Mercia in the mid-600s; Wulfric Spot, the founder of Burton Abbey; and Wulfstan, a Bishop of Worcester and later an Archbishop of York (1002) who wrote the 'Sermon of the Wolf to the English'. A handful of place names also incorporate the name wolf. Wolvey in Warwickshire means the enclosure protected against wolves, whilst in the same county Great and Little Wolford signify the place protected against wolves. And in the Black Country, Wordsley could be derived from the Anglo-Saxon word wulfweard, meaning wolf guard.

The first written record we have of Wordsley dates from the twelfth century when it was given as Wuluardeslea – a tongue twister for speakers of modern English. This spelling may also suggest that Wordsley might have a different origin, coming from the word wulfweardes, which would indicate the wood or clearing of a man called Wulfweard.

Whatever the exact derivation of its name, for centuries Wordsley was part of the large parish of Kingswinford – itself originally Svinesford, the pig ford, and which later gained the prefix King when it became a royal manor. Eleven square miles in area, Kingswinford incorporated a number of settlements, including Brierley Hill which was to become a major presence in the Black Country.

A painting from about 1840 showing the furnace inside the Richardson glass cone at the Wordsley Glassworks. Thanks to the Broadfield House Glass Museum.

Kingswinford is noted several times in Robert Plot's *The Natural History of Staffordshire* of 1686. In particular, he mentioned a spring near Ashwood Bridge; and the tile house at Bromley where John Heydon made steel. As for Wordsley, it is not mentioned in *Shaw's History and Antiquities of Staffordshire* (1801) and it receives but one brief reference in the *Curiosities of Dudley and the Black Country from 1800-1860* by C.F. G. Clarke (1881). Under 1832 it stated that:

At the time the late Mr. Thomas Hawkes won his first political spurs, as M.P. for old Dudley; he was the head of the glass trade in this town, and we could then boast of having *five large glass houses* in full operation in our midst, employing at the time upwards of 1,000 hands. Since that time the glass trade has nearly departed from Dudley, and we have now only one glass works amongst us—viz., that highly respectable firm of Messrs. John Eenaud and Son, at the foot of Tower Street, once the celebrated firm of Messrs. Guest, Wood and Guest. The glass trade seems to have migrated to Wordsley and Brettell Lane, for that is now a large centre of glass manufactory.

In 1834 William White in his History, Gazeteer and Directory of Staffordshire devoted a whole section to Kingswinford. He wrote that it was a small but pleasant village, with many neat houses that gave its name to a very extensive parish of over 15,000 folk, the greater portion of which was at Brierley Hill, Wordsley, Brettell Lane, Brockmoor, Bromley, Delph, Shutt End and Wall Heath. In these villages and hamlets were to be found many coal, iron and glass works, as well as a wire mill, nine potteries of stone and coarse black ware, several brick and tile yards, and a number of chain and nail manufacturers.

Later on, White explained that Saint Mary's Church in Kingswinford itself was now too small for the rapidly expanding population and so a handsome new church had been consecrated at Wordsley, "a modern village one mile to the south", which also boasted an Independent Chapel whose minister was the Reverend Jonah Bossano. Two flint glass manufactories were to be found at Wordsley, "one of which (Messrs. Webb and Richardson's) is said to be the oldest in the county."

As early as 1349, Edward III had ordered the purchase of glass in Staffordshire, although it would seem that then and for several generations thereafter the glass trade was focused upon Abbots Bromley and later Eccleshall. However, by the end of the 1620s, the industry had moved its centre to the Stourbridge district. This shift was associated with Paul Tyzack, one of a family of glaziers from Lorraine in France, who claimed to have invented the making of glass with coal instead of charcoal – a claim disputed by Dud Dudley.

Be that as it may, Tyzack made his home in Kingswinford, although his glass house was at Hungry Hill in Stourbridge. His presence drew in other Huguenot

*A photo of the Red House glassworks from the Gentleman's Magazine of 1902.
Thanks to the Broadfield House Glass Museum. The cone is 90 foot high and 60 foot
in diameter.*

(French Protestant) families from Lorraine who had fled from religious persecution in their homeland, although it is likely that as important an attraction for them was Amblecote fireclay - which made the best pots for glasshouses. Amongst these Lorrainers was Joshua Henzey who set up a glass house on coal bearing land in Brettell Lane.

The earliest glass house in Wordsley seems to have been Audnam at Audenham Bank. This was built in 1662 by Edward Bradley the elder, a white glass maker. It was later run by the Grazebrook family which concentrated upon flint glass production. This included flint and lead, which ensured a glass that was strong, heavy and bright. Gradually the lead content was increased and sand replaced flints, although the name fling glass stuck.

In the later eighteenth century, the Grazebrooks paid Lord Dudley £53 a year for the lease of the glass house with furnaces, mill house, warehouses and other buildings. All maintenance and repairs were undertaken by the lessee at his own cost.

A craftsman shaping the glass after he has gathered the metal (molten glass) from the pot on his hollow blowpipe, in 1902. Thanks to the Broadfield House Glass Museum.

Brewery Street ready for the carnival in 1930. Thanks to Malcolm Penn. The little girl is Jean Whitehouse aged three. In the doorway below the shop are Mrs King and her daughter, Nellie. Above the shop are Mr and Mrs Fletcher. Fry's Diecastings Works later occupied this site until the 1990s, when new houses were built here.

In 1704 the trade in Wordsley expanded when Thomas Henzey opened the Dial. This was a glass house that made broad glass, used for window glass. Broad glass was made by blowing cylinders of glass which were then slit and flattened on a table. It then had to be annealed, ground and polished. However, Henzey started production when this glass was losing favour to crown glass, which was thinner and brighter and was made from a large globe that was flashed into a circular disk which could be cut up into panes. Eventually sheet glass making replaced that of broad glass at the Dial.

The centre of each glass works was the coal-burning furnace, the upper part of which had a low-shallow-domed chamber in which were set the clay pots in which the glass was melted. The glassmakers worked around the furnace, gathering the molten glass from the pots via openings into which they inserted their irons. These men were split into teams, known as chairs. There were four to a chair: the gaffer or workman; the servitor; the foot maker; and the taker-in. Each had a different and important responsibility in the making of glass.

By the late 1700s there were seven glass houses in the Stourbridge area, two of which were in Wordsley and were run by R. Bradley and Ensor. Together they had 20 pots, more than anywhere else locally. It was in this period that the art of cutting and engraving glass was brought from Germany, first to London and then the Stourbridge district.

In the nineteenth century, the glass trade was invigorated by the repeal of the excise duty on glass in 1845. Six years later Richardson's of Wordsley exhibited at the Great Exhibition, although in the Catalogue to 'The Industry of all Nations' it was stated the firm was from Stourbridge – probably because this was a better known place.

The Catalogue informed readers that Richardson's was chiefly famous for crystal glass:

which they have carried to the utmost extent of brilliancy and purity. An examination of their contributions in decanters, wine-glasses, goblets, cream-bowls, butter-coolers etc will at once carry conviction that in this branch of the art England excels every other country of the world. Bohemia asserts, and probably maintains, its supremacy in the manufacture of coloured glass, but it cannot enter into com petition with us as regards that which is colourless.

Margaret Broome, then aged 66, and eighteen year old Julia Hall looking at photos and illustrations of Wordsley past and present at an exhibition at Wordsley Community Centre in March 1981. The exhibition coincided with the reopening of the centre's annexe at Richardson Hall after a £22,000 facelift.

In addition to their crystal, Richardson's also made the glass for candle lamps exhibited by Blews and Sons of Birmingham.

Later in the nineteenth century, Richardson's and the Webbs of the Platts, Amblecote brought back to life the ancient Roman art of cameo glass, sculpturing glass by hand. One of the most talented exponents of this intricate process was John Northwood, who was crucial in the reproduction of the Portland Vase. This was the most famous and most influential piece of glass from the ancient world. Almost ten inches high, its cobalt blue background is enhanced by opaque white human and imaginative figures and objects cut in a cameo relief. The original had been smashed in 1845, although it was to be repaired three times, and the reproduction took three years to complete.

Northwood carved the cameo at his own workshop in Wordsley, but the replica itself was blown by Daniel Hancock at the nearby Red House Glassworks. Built between 1788 and 1794 by Richard Bradley close to the Stourbridge Canal Navigation and the new road from Stourbridge to Wolverhampton, it became indelibly associated with Stuart Crystal.

In 1827, eleven-year old Frederick Stuart from Codsall started as a clerk at the glass works. Twenty-five years later, Stuart joined other partners to form the Albert Glassworks next to the Red House. They built the last cone in the area. Manufacturers of table glassware and crystal chandeliers, in 1867 Stuart and Mills supplied the famed steamship, the 'Great Eastern' – which was so connected with the rise of Tangye's of Smethwick. Frederick Stuart then went on to lease the Red House and thereafter the building remained with the family.

Stuart's kept secret the exact composition of its crystal, but the firm's brochure in 1934 explained that it was consisted approximately of 55% silica, 33% lead oxide and 12% potassium oxide. These ingredients were weighed carefully and then put into a large drum which mixed them by rotating. Once this was done the batch was ready for melting.

The Red House glass cone was used until 1936 and was Grade 2 Listed thirty years later. Later restored, the Red House glass cone is now a superb visitor attraction and it is the only complete glass gone left locally and is one of only four in the United Kingdom. As the best preserved of these, the cone is one of the most important industrial buildings in Britain. A feature of the British glass industry, cones acted as a huge chimney for the furnace, drawing in air through underground tunnels to enable a sufficiently high temperature to melt the glass. They also served as a working space for the glassmakers.

The Red House Glass Cone brings to the fore the talents of so many Black Country glassmakers. Men such as Charles Stanier, district secretary of the Flint Glassmakers' Society and afterwards the glassmaking instructor at the Stourbridge School of Arts and Crafts. Men such as Stan Gill, who was an apprentice at Richardson's before joining Stuart's about 1930. And men like Bonnie Nicklin, who started as a glassmaker in Dudley aged eleven and became one of the foremost glassmakers at Stuart's, receiving the BEM in 1948 for his achievements as a craftsman.

Located on the main road to Stourbridge, the Red House glass cone was joined by the White House and Wordsley Flint Glass Works, also known as the London House because it supplied the trade in the capital. Both are now gone. Once glass cones dominated the Wordsley skyline and proclaimed its significance to the world of glass making. Despite its small population, just under 6,000 in 1901, Wordsley was a place of renown. The Red House glass cone ensures that neither Wordsley nor its glassmakers will be forgotten.

Colin Finch of Cefn Fforest, Blackwood, has read the recent article on the glass industry at Wordsley. There were many names in it that he remembered, "as I am a former employee of Stuart Crystals, at the Redhouse glass works at Wordsley, but with a difference - I worked in the Welsh factory at Pengam, and grew from shop floor glass making to General production Manager, between 1971-1989.

"There are many stories that I could tell you about these characters none more so that Mr Stan Gill, who was a legend in his own life time. The finest glass maker the trade has ever seen. He had the most wonderful hands and the finest gift a glass maker could have, in making his work look easy. My first encounter with Stan was as a 17 year old young apprentice on a visit to Stuart's from the Pengam factory. I watched in awe of this little gentleman walking across RED carpet, in bedroom slippers warming a piece of glass in his glory hole, before shearing and removing the top ready for shaping. I was dumbstruck to say the least.

"I know many of hundreds of glass makers and decorators in the Stourbridge area from a long period of time and enjoyed many traditional Black Country nights out with great men at pubs such as the Black Cat, the Vine, The Bell in Market Street, the Dudley Arm's, Nine Locks Inn and many more.

"The men of my generation were people like John Wale; John Measse (sadly deceased); Roger Sidaway; Reg Everton; former general secretary of the glass and flintstone workers union Mr Jack Price; its former president Billy Evans, one of the finest statesman I ever had the privilege to have worked with; and towards the end of my career, Lawson Hill of Webb Corbet. The list could go on and on and on.

"Carl, as a devoted Welshman the only other place in this country there are men of the same quality as the Welsh are the Glass makers and decorators of the Black Country."

Many of the photos in this chapter are taken from an important new book by Stan Hill called Wordsley Past and Present (Sutton Publishing, £12.99). Stan is an extraordinary man who has made a major impact upon our understanding of the history of the Black Country and our appreciation of its significance. Qualifying as a teacher in 1948, he developed a pioneering local studies course at Audnam Secondary

School with Mr D. R. Guttery, a well-known local historian and chairman of the school governors. For much of the 1950s, Stan was also active in municipal life as a councillor on Brierley Hill Urban District Council, for which authority he was chairman in 1955-56.

After moving on to teaching posts in Smethwick, Walsall and Dudley, Stan became Warden of the new Dudley Teachers' Centre at Himley Hall in 1969. He supposedly retired in 1988 and was invited to succeed Harold Parsons, the founder editor of The Blackcountryman, the quarterly magazine of the Black Country Society. Since then Stan has become a true ambassador for the region he loves, giving numerous talks, interviewing scores of local people, and editing 53 issues of this vital magazine before passing on the editorship in 2001.

The author of two books on Brierley Hill and of several other works, he has been helped in his publication on Wordsley by Fred Willetts. Fred is a past chairman and president of the Wordsley History Society and is its custodian of over 1,000 slides of old Wordsley. Stan continues to work unstintingly for the good of the Black Country Society and of the Black Country in general. I pay tribute to his determination and dedication and salute him for his unselfish devotion to the people of the Black Country.

Chapter 6

NUTS AND BOLTS CENTRE OF THE WORLD: DARLASTON

As if standing guard, a line of hills stretches across the south of the Black Country, dominating the landscape. Rising up just below Wolverhampton, they line up in a south-easterly fashion beginning with Sedgley Beacon and moving on through the Wren's Nest, and Dudley Castle Hill to the Rowley Hills. The high ground then marches onward, although more narrowly and less pronounced, out of the Black Country and across Quinton and Frankley Beeches, going on to merge with the ridges of Clent and Lickey.

Important for their limestone and road metal, these hills were vital to the industrial development of the Black Country and they lie on the watershed of England. To the west, water drains to the River Severn via the Smestow and Stour system; whilst to the east the River Tame and its small tributaries flow away to the River Trent and the North Sea.

World renowned for their geology and fossils, these hills provide a magnificent vantage point for the South Staffordshire Plateau. Standing up on Kates Hill at night and looking north-eastwards, down at the valley of the River Tame, the darkness is picked out by a multitude of lights from countless homes and factories in an almost magical illumination.

In the daylight, it is clear that this low-lying ground is broken up by low hills formed in most cases by glacial drift and which have not been eroded by streams. From early times, these hills in the basin of the upper Tame attracted settlers, but the names that we call them today are those given them by the Angles who moved in to what is now the West Midlands in the late sixth and seventh centuries.

There's Bilston, mentioned in Lady Wulfrun's charter of 985 and a few years later in 996 when it was given as Bilsetnatun, meaning the farmstead or estate – tun - of the dwellers on the sharp ridge – bill saete. Then there's Wednesbury, bringing to mind Woden, the greatest of the old pagan gods, who was the creator, the god of victory and of the dead and who is also remembered in Wednesday. Signifying the stronghold – burgh – of Woden, Wednesbury may not have been mentioned in documents until the Domesday Book of 1086 but its name indicates a much older origin.

Lying between these two is another hill settlement, that of Darlaston. Just over a mile north west of Wednesbury and three miles south west of Walsall, it is also unnamed in the unprecedented and massive gathering of information ordered by William the Conqueror – unlike the other Darlaston in Staffordshire near to Stone. Mind you, that is not to say that there was no Darlaston in the aftermath of the Norman Conquest. It may have been included within a bigger manor, such as that of Sedgley, or a scribe may have missed it out by mistake. We don't know. What we can say is that Darlaston signifies the estate (tun) of Deorlaf.

A street trader selling his goods in Pinfold Street, Darlaston in the late nineteenth century. I thank Howard Madeley for allowing me to use this and the other photos on Darlaston. Howard was one of two men who founded what is now the thriving Darlaston Local History Society. A pioneer in promoting the history of the town, Howard has worked unstintingly to ensure that the history of Darlaston is passed on and that its people will not be forgotten. Generous with sharing his research and photos, Howard is the epitome of what a local historian should be – committed, persevering, sensitive to the past, thorough in his research and proud of his locality.

The earliest document for the place named it as Derlaveston in 1262, although by 1316 its modern form had emerged when it was recorded as Derlaston. According to Sampson Erdeswicke, whose pioneering and unpublished survey of Staffordshire was carried out over the decade from 1593, a William of Darlaston was lord of the manor at about the time of Henry III, who reigned for much of the thirteenth century. In 1801, the Reverend Stebbing Shaw brought out an indispensable tome on the *History and Antiquities of Staffordshire*, drawing on the work of Erdeswick and others. Fortunately he brought to light a little more information on the history of Darlaston.

The first deed that he mentioned related to Thomas Lord of Darlaston transferring to Hugh son of John de Bylestone a messuage (a dwelling house and its surrounding property, including and outbuildings) formerly held by Amice le Peynnereste. Shaw thought that this document also came from the reign of Henry III, and in another deed he noted that a wood belonging to a William de Darlaston had been destroyed of old. The direct line of the Darlastons later died out and for a time their old possession came into the hands of Henry VIII when it was valued at thirteen pounds nine shillings and thruppence farthing.

Still, despite Shaw's researches, there is little hard information about Darlaston and its history. In Robert Plot's *Natural History of Staffordshire* in 1686 it merited but a handful of references. One related to the local iron ore which could be made into nails, whilst another praised the generosity of a Dr Thomas Pye. Born in Darlaston, he was educated at Oxford and became a vicar, teacher and writer in Sussex who was noted for his learning. In 1606, Pye visited "some Relations at Darlaston near Wednesbury, upon occasion that some of his Servants going to ring in the old Steeple which was of wood and weak, had been in danger of their lives". Accordingly, Pye offered to pay for a tower of stone for the parish church of Saint Lawrence so long as the people of the "town" paid for its transport. This they did and also put up an inscription to his good-heartedness and piety.

Such references to Darlaston are rare. Too often it was overlooked by commentators or else it was associated with Wednesbury and given no clear identity of its own. However, in 1698, good coal mines were pointed out at Darlaston. It is not surprising for it lies above the Middle Coal Measures of the South Staffordshire coal field, where the Thick Coal is rarely more than 400 feet below the surface.

Shaw himself was alert to the importance of coal to Darlaston. He wrote that

there are several coal-pits sunk lately, and probably will soon be more, as they have lately cut a canal through the parish to Walsall. There is only one coal mine at which they work now in this parish, in which the coal is about 7 yards thick. The ironstone is about three quarters of a yard thick, and is found in the parish under the coal. The mines are very subject to damps. The miners are subject to asthmatic complaints, and very few of them live to be seventy years of age. The air is sharp and dry. There is great plenty of brick, tile and quarry clay; in some places not more than 4 feet, and in others a great deal more. There is a mine of clay now at work in which they have gone 13 or 14 feet deep, and it is then good. They are prevented going deeper by water.

In addition to the miners and quarrymen, there were numerous gun lock makers and nailers in the locality.

By 1801, Darlaston had a population of about 3,000 people living in 600 houses. Its area was small, encompassing just over 1,500 acres and it ranged two miles east to west and one and a quarter miles north to south. Of this total there were about 800 acres of arable and pasture, upon which wheat, barley and oats were generally grown, and 30 acres of meadow. Amongst the chief buildings were the church, its schools opened in 1793, a meeting house for the "very numerous" Methodists dating back to 1762, and another place of worship for the Independents "who are very few".

In the succeeding years, Darlaston continued to be ignored by observers. *The Strangers Guide to Modern Birmingham* published in 1825 belied its title by including material on many Black Country towns, but its entry for Darlaston was

Workers at F. H. Lloyd in Darlaston, with some of their sons in the front row holding the dinner they have been sent with during their dinner time from school.

brief. The writer declared that the place was only one mile distant from Wednesbury and that "neither on the road or in the village could I perceive any thing deserving of attention; the inhabitants being employed in the same pursuits as at Wednesbury". These included coal mining, the gun trade, the making of springs, steps and other articles for coach makers and the production of "wood screws, hinges, and of late, apparatus for the gas lights".

Nine years later, in his *History, Gazetteer and Directory of Staffordshire* of 1834 William White explained that "the manufacture of the place is gunlocks; and there are several steel furnaces and forges for the supply of steel for the locks and springs that are made". The British gun trade was focused upon Birmingham and was marked out by its sub-divisions. One of these was the making of locks, most of which came from Darlaston and Wednesbury.

During the long French Wars from 1791-1815, the gun lock makers of Darlaston prospered. In 1838, a short but interesting account of them was given in *Osborne's Guide to the Grand Junction Railway*, which line passed just to the east of the town and stopped at James's Bridge. The writer stressed that during the war:

> a good workman could get a pound note per day. Granting a considerable allowance for the depreciation of paper money, yet the profitable employment in making gun locks was such, that by working only two days a week, the men could obtain as much as would supply their wants, and find them the means of enjoying the only luxury they seemed to know - that of drinking four days a week - which they used to indulge, out of loyalty to their own country, and hatred to France.

Like most middle-class writers, this person pandered to the predilection of middle-class readers for shocking accounts of working-class behaviour. He relished in reinforcing negative stereotypes of working-class people, deploring the way that "these Darlaston gun lock makers used to live in the most luxurious and extravagant manner. Such was their demand for poultry, fish, and meat, that Darlaston became the most profitable market for these things in the neighbourhood."

Appalled that working-class people should have the temerity to earn good money and to enjoy themselves, the writer fulminated that the workers "might have made fortunes in the days of prosperity, but they not only spent what they obtained extravagantly, but refused to work more than one or two days a week. During this belligerent carnival the people sunk even lower than before in vice and immorality, and not one particle of what can be denominated personal or household comfort, was obtained. Bull-baiting, dog and cockfighting, and all sorts of low and debased practices, were the amusements they indulged in, while swearing, cursing, and disgustingly foul language, seemed to grow with their prosperity."

Darlaston Green, formerly, Upper Green, in the Mid-1960s. The top of Booth Street is on the left.

It is noteworthy that the writer paid no attention to the drinking, gambling, carousing, cock fighting and fox hunting of the upper class. Be that as it may, he did acknowledge that "the workmen are incredibly ingenious, being able to forge almost anything on the anvil". So they could. Until the late 1850s, lock making was a hand trade and according to the 1866 account of John Goodman of the Birmingham Small Arms Company, "the several parts of each lock were forged on the anvil by men whose wonderful skill became proverbial". These various parts were put together by filers and were finished by polishing and hardening.

The coming of peace in 1815 led to a depression generally in Britain. In particular, it brought a marked decline in the fortunes of the Darlaston gun lock makers. Despite this the trade remained an important one. By 1861 there were five or six main workshops in the town, each employing about 20 skilled men; and there were between 20 and 30 little masters. However, because of mechanisation and the emergence of gun production in other countries the end was fast approaching for the trade,

In 1865, Jones's *Mercantile Directory of the Iron District* included 26 gun lock makers, forgers or filers - one of whom was a woman, Ellen Butler a gun lock forger and stamper of Wolverhampton Lane. Several were also shopkeepers or publicans. Their need for an alternative income highlighted the adverse conditions for those involved in making gun locks by hand.

The final blow came in the depression which afflicted gunmaking after the end of the Franco-Prussian War in 1876. Within fifteen years the gun lock trade had disappeared from Darlaston. Some of those who lost their jobs were taken on by the BSA in Birmingham, but understandably they found it hard to cast off their craft. Their foreman stated that they followed the practices of a hundred years previously, bow and breast drilling instead of using power machinery, whilst they continued to buy their own tallow-dip candles instead of the best Russian tallow free supplied by the company. Furthermore they "would do no more tempering after ten o'clock in the morning, owing to their superstitious belief ... that springs tempered after that hour would break".

The sad fate of these Darlaston men was that of all skilled workers whose craft was destroyed by mechanisation and it was shared by the nailers of the town whose trade became extinct in the same years. The harsh economic conditions were made worse by the closing of local mines and the collapse in the 1880s of two major employers: Bills and Mills, which embraced blast furnaces, foundries, metal processing, and coal mines; and Addenbrooke, Smith and Pidcock, coal and iron masters.

Battered by hard times, Darlaston's population fell from 14,739 in 1871 to 13,900 ten years later. Fortunately new jobs soon arose because of the adaptability

Campbell Place, Darlaston in 1965. The street was named after Colonel J. V. Campbell, VC, CMG, DSO. The Peters family of sign writers lived in the shop in the centre.

of some of the town's gun lock makers, such as William Wilkes of Eldon Street. By 1865, he had also moved into the production of nuts and bolts – as had John Archer and Son of Great Croft Street and Pinfold Street. There were another fifteen businesses involved in this trade. They laid the foundation for Darlaston to push itself to the fore as the nuts and bolts capital of the world.

For many years, this industry was characterised by small-scale operations. In 1851 Alexander Cotterill was the largest employer with just fourteen men. A decade later he had expanded to give work to 75, but within a few years such a number had been dwarfed by those employed in large factories. By 1911, between six and thousand people were engaged in making nuts and bolts in the Black Country, the great majority of them in Darlaston. Perhaps half of them were employed by Guest Keen and Nettlefold's, which had taken over the Atlas Works at the turn of the twentieth century.

Until 1890, places such as this had supplied nuts and bolts for railways in the British Empire. As this market dropped off, massive demand came first from the rapidly expanding electrical engineering and machine-tool trades and second, after 1900, from the motor industry.

Another proud Darlaston company also pushed itself into the limelight in this period through its innovation, design and quality products. It was Rubery Owen. Back in 1834 a Jabez Rubery had been a gun lock filer, screw turner and gun lock maker. Fifty years the brothers J. T. and T. W. Rubery had started a factory in Booth Street for making light steel roof work, fencing, gates and the occasional bridge. Later T. W. Rubery left the business, and in 1893 his brother went into partnership with Alfred Ernest Owen.

A young engineer of talent, foresight and determination, Owen transformed the company. Alert to the rise of new industries and to the potential for supplying them with new products, he oversaw the making of an award-winning chassis frame for a car made from rolled sections and solid round steel bars.

In 1910 Owen became sole owner and with his acute vision he added an aviation department, so allowing Rubery Owen to supply small aircraft components in the First World War. By that time, his company was also making car wheels and had taken over Chains Limited of Wednesbury and Nuts and Bolts Ltd of Darlaston as well as two Birmingham businesses.

Alfred Ernest Owen died in 1929. He was followed ably by his two sons, Sir Alfred and E. W. B. They led a highly skilled, motivated workforce that helped the people of Darlaston withstand the ravages of the Depression of the 1930s and which played a vital role in the Second World War. Rubery Owen's structural department at Darlaston was responsible for building shadow factories, aircraft hangers, Bailey bridges, tank-landing craft and components for the Mulberry Harbours that were so essential to the success of the Normandy Landings.

During the same period, the motor-frame department made gun carriages, projectiles, mines and bomb-trolleys; the motor wheel department produced instrument containers, bomb carriers, anti-submarine weapons, bomb tails and much more; whilst the aviation department turned out nuts and bolts for aircraft.

After the war Rubery Owen continued to expand, but like all Black Country manufacturers it suffered badly because of the economic problems of the 1970s and unhappily its main plant closed in 1980. The year before the GKN factory had shut down. Just as a century earlier, Darlaston and its people were buffeted by a severe economic downturn. Unfortunately, unlike then no new industry appeared to provide manufacturing employment.

With the massive loss of jobs locally, the town centre also declined, but Darlaston and its folk are resilient and hardy, and are resolved to work for the best of their town. In the fore of that movement is the Darlaston Local History. They have striven to let younger generations know about the past of the town and have brought out a number of important publications. Their latest is edited by Tony Highfield and called *Stories of Darlaston*. Next week I shall bring you extracts from that book based on the reminiscences of people who

John Stackhouse of Knowles Street, Wednesbury thoughtfully sent in this photo of his sister, Kathy, who won the 1951 Darlaston Beauty Queen competition held at the Regal Picture House, Darlaston. The music was provided by Mr Leslie Taff, who used to play the organ at the Regal for the silent movies on the Regal's famous organ. John recalls that "Kathy was also presented with a cash prize by Sir Alfred Owen and a bouquet of flowers by actress Patricia Neale. She also won a designer dress from a top Birmingham ladies' fashion shop and a hair do from Evelyn Warner, ladies' hair dresser of Darlaston.

"Kathy's first assignment was to open Darlaston's sports day held at Herbert's Park. A. G. B. Owen together with the Wolves players of the day were in attendance. My eldest sister, Beryl, Kathy and myself lived in Hewitt Street, Darlaston. Kathy now lives on the Costa Blanca, Spain, with her husband, Peter Grafton."

have spent most of their lives living and working in a town whose history deserves to be drawn to wider attention. Darlaston, like all the Black Country towns, punched well above its weight for over a century on the world stage and through the ingenuity, innovation, adaptability, prowess and hard graft of its people it made the world take notice of itself. Let us hope that it can do so again.

There is a smashing new book edited by Tony Highfield and brought out by the Darlaston Local History Society. It is called *A Book for all the Family. Stories of Darlaston. Darlaston Through the Years*

It is packed with the memories of people who care deeply about Darlaston and who wish that the history of its people should be brought to the fore. Amongst the contributors is well-known Black Country author, Meg Hutchinson. Tony Highfield himself is ardent in his determination to make sure that Darlaston is not swept from history. His other publications include *Memories of Old Darlaston, Memories of Christmas* and *Memories of Billy Muggins.*

This last book ensures that the memory of one of Darlaston's best-loved characters is kept alive. Born William Walters in Eldon Street and later nicknamed Billy Muggins, this man of Darlaston traipsed the streets collecting scrap and was noted for playing his mouth organ and reciting the Scriptures.

I congratulate Tony and the Darlaston Local History Society for their sterling efforts to collect memories and photographs about Darlaston, for bringing out important books, and for providing a much-needed platform for the understanding of Darlaston's past.

Stories of Darlaston is priced at just £2.25 and is available from Darlaston Library at 1, King Street, Darlaston, Walsall, West Midlands, WS10 8DD. Telephone: 0121 526 4530; Fax: 0121 526 2298; and e-mail darlastonlibrary@walsall.gov.uk

The Darlaston Local History Society meets on the last Thursday of the month at 7.30 in the evening at Salter Street Methodist Hall. Everyone who has an interest and a passion for the history of Darlaston is welcome.

Chapter 7

ALL BAR THE SQUAYL: THE COOK SHOP, OLD HILL

All "bar the squayl", that's what the butchers and cooked meat specialists of the Black Country always said about a pig. They used all of it, all bar the squayl, and no truer saying was spoken. The pig was vital to the diet of working-class folk, from its trotters that were salted to its fat that made lard, and from its bones that were turned into a pie to its ears that were stuffed. And if there was something of the pig that you couldn't get down yer wassin, then it could be made use of in some other way. Its bristles might go into a brush or stitches for cobblers, whilst the fat from its intestines made a coarse grease for wheels.

Given its over-riding significance to the working-class household, the killing of a pig was a noteworthy affair. In the days before refrigeration and proper abattoirs, the pig would be killed in the cooler months of the year, between November and Easter. The autumn month was especially favoured because it was the time of the first frosts that heralded the cold season and which meant that the carcass could be chilled quickly. As well as that a pig killed in November would not need to be fed in the hard days of winter, whilst it would mean food for all the family not only for Christmas but also well into the new year.

The pig sticker may have been the local pork butcher or a handyman, or even the chap who owned the pig - if he was confident enough that he could do the job. Whoever it was, he was in charge of a ritual that went back donkeys' years. The day itself was chosen carefully and could not be when the moon was on the wane – because on such a day it was thought that the meat would shrink in weight in the brine tub. How the sticking of the pig went depended on the bloke in charge. He might have had a way with him, which allowed him to calm the pig. Stroking the animal and chatting with it, the more sensitive pig sticker would carefully dangle his noose of rope until he was able to slip it onto the pig's snout and lead it into the fode (yard). If there was a suff (drain) there, then that was all the better.

Mind you, on his own the pig sticker couldn't kill the animal. The pig might be around 300 pounds in weight. Big, strong and heavy, it took several fellers to push, pull and lift it on to its back or side and on to a low wooden bench. Sometimes called a cratch or stool, this had two legs and a pair of handles at each end. The pig's feet were tied to the handles, its head was drawn back by the rope, and then it was stuck by plunging a knife into its jugular vein. If there was no cratch, then the pig was killed while standing or lying on straw.

Not that the killing of the pig always went smoothly. Often the pig was dragged from its sty squealing and thrusting itself hither and thither with fright. Many's the time the enraged and fearful animal forced itself out of the grip of its captors and raced around the fode in a hopeless attempt to escape. But always it was overpowered by the men and brought back to the cratch ready for the knife. It was believed that the pig should not be stuck too deeply for it had to die slowly so that the meat would be well bled.

So soon as ever it was stuck, and as it gave out its last despairing wails, the blood sprang out from its throat and was collected in basins so as to be used to make black pudding. A little salt was added to prevent thickening and later groats were put into the mix along with breadcrumbs, milk, thyme and other spices, suet, pork fat and eggs. Once the last of the blood had been collected then the bristles were removed from the body. This was done by scalding the carcass with hot water and then scraping it with a knife, or by singeing it with burning straw. Afterwards, slits were cut into the back part of the hind legs so that a piece of wood could be wedged between them to allow the carcass to be hung from big hooks in the brew'us (wash-house). This allowed the pig killer to cut open the animal and take out its innards, amongst which were its heart, lungs, liver, kidneys and blether - bladder, which was blown up and used for a football. In the Black Country this offal was caught in a mill pon – a large pan. Another bowl was put beneath the carcass to catch hold of the last of the blood.

The day after the killing, the pig killer cut up the carcass, but by then the offal had already been turned into food. Chitalins, chitterlings, were the smaller intestines. They were cleaned thoroughly in running water and were then plaited, boiled in salted water and cooled. These would be served with a little malt vinegar and a piece or two with marg, or they were cut into small pieces and fried with sliced onions. A stock was then added and thickened with cornflour to make a nice gravy. The glands from the neck and stomach were also used. Soaked in cold water to remove membranes and skin, these sweetbreads were boiled in water and, after draining, were fried or braised.

And then, of course, there were faggots. Made with pig's fry, onions, sage, breadcrumbs, salt and pepper and served with a gravy made of water and cornflower, each faggot ball was wrapped in a caul or kell. This was the lacy, fatty membrane of the stomach and guts and it kept the faggots moist during cooking. Each Black Country mother seemed to have her own special way of making faggots, but as industrialisation swept across the region not all mothers were in a position to make their own faggots and such like. The overpowering desire of manufacturing for workers drew women as much as men into workshops and factories and many wives found it hard to find the time to work at making chains, nails, metal bits and other tough jobs and to make hot meals each night. And whilst pig keeping remained common, not every household was now able to rear its pig. In these circumstances little cook shops began to appear.

Once they abounded across both the Black Country and Brummagem, selling not only faggots and peas but also tripe and onions and other tasty, cheap and filling dishes such as grorty dick and grey pays and bercun. It was regular sight to see youngsters traipsing down to the cook shop on a Friday night with a jug or basin to fetch these Black Country take-aways, that is until the social and economic changes of the 1960s and 1970s destroyed so much of traditional working-class life. Slowly, the cook shops closed down and faded away, but that heritage of Black Country cooking did not disappear completely. It is kept alive in one thriving place. Old Hill still boasts its cook shop, and it is simply called that. The Cook Shop is run by Nigel Brazier (although he'd be lost without the ladies who work with him!) and this month he and his family are celebrating 115 years of serving Black Country food to Black Country folk.

The family's bond with cooking food for people to take home goes back four generations to Eve Billingham, Nigel's great grandmother. She and her chap lived with their children in High Street, Old Hill (now Highgate Street because of a perverse name change imposed by outsiders on the local people). Like many an enterprising mother, Eve decided to bring in a few extra shillings for the family by turning her front room into a shop and providing wholesome dinners for those women who were wacked out by their hard collar and who needed to get something hot, on the table for the old mon and kids.

Married first to Arthur Billingham, with whom she had three wenches and a lad, and later to Harry Shaw from Hednesford,

Eve Billingham, who began the Cook Shop story in 1889, with her fourth child, Arthur.

Eve was the first woman in her family to become a shopkeeper. Strong and determined, she made what her customers wanted and what she could cook: faggots and peas, chitterlings, ham hocks, pig's trotters and fresh bread – for what good was a good meal without a fresh piece? Mind you, it wasn't easy. The three girls, Mary, Amy and Jessie, slept top and tail and "fust up was best dressed". All three had to help with the shop and make deliveries to customers in a three-wheeled basket carriage. In later years, Amy married a tailor and Jessie became a successful businesswoman. She had "a penchant for champagne, designer clothes and diamonds funded by her exclusive millinery shops in Walsall and Hednesford. She styled herself as 'Estelle' and died a very rich woman and left it all to charity." As for Mary, she married Joe Priest. A proper Black Country mon who knew how to graft, Joe was one of thirteen children, but he and Mary just had the one babby – Iris.

By 1922, Joe was working as a puddler at Hingley's Ironworks in Cox's Lane. On one occasion he needed a new pair of moleskin trousers, which were hardwearing and gave some protection from the spitting of the molten iron with which he worked. His wife Mary was loath to discard the old pair and as her grandson Nigel recalls, she "decided she would patch them but for some reason known only to herself she cut the patch from the new pair of trousers! This idiosyncratic behaviour is typical of the women in our family..."

The 1920s were hard years for the working class. So many people had hoped for a land fit for heroes after the end of the First World War but their high expectations were dashed upon the rocks of an economic downturn. In the Black Country, as elsewhere in Britain, the old industries went into decline. Miners, chainmakers and ironworkers by the thousand were laid off. Joe Priest was one of them. When he signed on at the Labour, he was told that if he emigrated to Canada his

Mary and Joe Priest in the mid-1920s in Linton Road, Old Hill before they started their own Cook Shop.

passage would be paid for and a job would await him. Once he was settled he could send for his wife and daughter. Mary herself was only seven but remembers listening with tears in her eyes as her mom and dad discussed what they should do. Fortunately they resolved to stay put and make a go of it by opening their own cook shop in Halesowen Road, Old Hill.

It was demanding work. Mary and Joe started at 8 in the morning and went on to a quarter to eleven at night Monday to Friday and to midnight on a Saturday. On Sunday they attended Saint James's Chapel, Old Hill – known locally as the 'Rhubarb Chapel'. With Mary taking the lead, the two of them did well selling faggots and peas made to her mother's recipe and pork sandwiches, fruit cakes, cups of tay, chitterlings and hocks.

Things picked up and the couple decided to pay someone to paint the front of their shop. The timing was not good as it coincided with a ha'penny rise in their pies, the first in the five years since they had started. In a region devastated by the Depression and across which stalked the spectre of the Means Test Man, some of

Joe Priest working at the present Cook Shop in 1962 when he was 67.

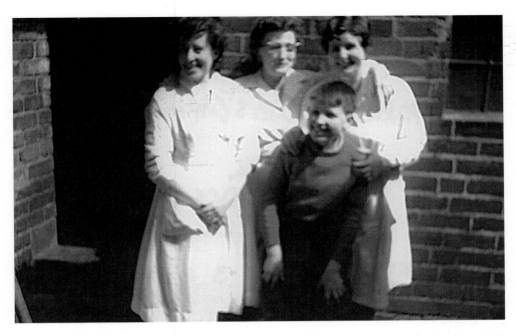

At the rear of the present Cook Shop in 1962 are Mary Parker, Iris Brazier (middle), Sue Tommy and Nigel Brazier aged thirteen. Sue Tommy is now 93 and worked for three generations of Cook Shop owners.

the customers were angered. They threatened to boycott that shop because "Yo med all o' that outa we!" And when Mary and Joe managed to save up for a week's holiday there were mutterings of, "Yo cor be doin too bad if yo con shurrup for a wick". That holiday was spent in the nearby Clent Hills, the playground of the Black Country, and a life-long friendship was struck up with Mrs Beddall who ran a bed and breakfast at Church Farm.

At the age of fourteen, Iris left school and like many a Black Country young woman she was found a job in Birmingham, where firms like Lucas's, the Austin and GEC were taking on workers. Iris herself went to work at Larkin's Warehouse in Livery Street and it was there that she met her husband-to-be, Bill Brazier. After four years, Iris left Larkin's and joined her mom and dad in the Cook Shop. Just eighteen, she and Bill decided to marry. Bill was in the Worcestershire Regiment stationed at the Norton Barracks in Worcester. It was early summer 1940, not long after the evacuation of the British Expeditionary Force from Dunkirk, and Bill was confined to barracks. All he had was his battledress, but with church booked Mrs Beddall drove to Worcester with her husband's raincoat and trousers in the boot. Bill managed to get changed and made it to Old Hill Church for the wedding on

Nigel Brazier taking out the faggots at the Cook Shop.

Saturday 22 June. The newlyweds had one night's honeymoon in Clent and then Bill was driven back to his barracks. An honest chap, he owned up and was given seven days in jankers for being Absent Without Leave.

Although rationing was widespread during the war, many of the Cook Shop's products did not need coupons and so demand was great. By the time Mary and Joe opened up at eight in the morning some folk had been queuing for two hours, and by eleven o'clock they were sold out. Luckily Joe had contacts with local farmers and was able to keep meat coming in, more so than they should have had according to the books!

Like so many Black Country folk, Joe and Mary still kept a pig in the fode of the Cook Shop "and every eight months the unfortunate pig (which was for some inexplicable reason always called 'Queenie') trotted down the road to be replaced immediately by a new piglet". One year, Joe had a bet with his best pal, George Patrick, a butcher with a shop at the bottom of High Street, Old Hill. Both of them had a piglet from the same litter and wagered on which one would rear the biggest and fattest when killed and dressed out.

Joe's wife loved all animals, but she had a special fondness for pigs. Unaware of the bet, Mary lavished care and attention on Queenie, which was fed with choice tit bits from the shop. One Sunday when Joe was out, Mary opened a tin of peaches and a tin of fussel's cream for tea. Unable to eat all of it she took the leftovers out to Queenie. It was raining and, mindful of the pig's comfort, Mary draped it in her best embroidered tablecloth. Queenie walloped down the peaches and cream and then got stuck into the table cloth. When Joe came back he copped out because it was his idea to have a pig! Any road up, by the time Queenie was slaughtered this pig was "the size of a fat donkey and weighed 20 score pounds when dressed out. Joe won the bet by a margin of 120lbs!"

Mary retired in 1949 but Joe carried on in the Cook Shop. Four years later their daughter Iris and son-in-law Bill opened their own cook shop six doors down. The family agreed that each shop would sell different products. Joe carried on with hot pork sandwiches, pies and faggots, whilst Iris and Bill focused on cooked meats and

sweet pastries. At last in 1959, Joe packed up and went to work with Iris and Bill. They were joined in 1965 by their son, Nigel, who had learned to take orders at the 'Lyttleton Arms' in Hagley. Despite being outnumbered by three men, Iris remained the gaffer.

Eventually, Joe retired in 1960 and gradually Nigel was allowed to take over the running of the shop. He was the first male member of the family to do so and for this he was given the title of 'honorary woman' by many of the customers! Nigel continues to make bostin pork cobs with his gran's special, secret recipe stuffing, and mouth-watering fruit pies, groaty pudding, faggots and peas, chitterlings, hams, brawn, chawl, cooked pies, and much more. Like all small businesses, the Cook Shop faces difficult trading conditions but it remains more than just a shop. It is a centre of the community and of Black Country culture. Like his great grandmother, gran and mom, Nigel is proud to serve the people of the West Midlands and to keep alive our region's distinctive dishes.

Bill Brazier at Clent on Remembrance Sunday 2000. Bill's birthday was 6 June, D Day, and he landed on the beaches on D Day plus 4 in 1944. Bill died as this article went out in the Express and Star and I dedicate it to his memory.

Chapter 8

WODEN'S FORT, COAL AND IRON: WEDNESBURY

It is one of the most impressive vantage points in the Black Country, the hill from which rises Saint Bartholomew's, the parish church of Wednesbury, or the black church as some call it. A proud building, it dominates the area, standing as it does upon a steep hill that is 537 feet above sea level. Half way between Junctions 8 and 9 of the M6, tens of thousands of people speed by it each day on their journeys up and down the country, but how few of them ever wonder about the history of this church and of the town to which it belongs.

An outcrop from the valley of the Tame, Church Hill is a tremendous vantage point and gives stunning views to the south. Down below are Tipton, Oldbury and other low-lying Black Country settlements and beyond them can be seen the Rowley-Northfield Ridge, on the water shed of England. Noticeable landmarks on this high ground are the keep of Dudley Castle, Sedgley Beacon and the Rowley Hills. With such an outlook and such a defensive position, it is little wonder that stories abound that Wednesbury traces its roots deep into history.

Many people believe that there was an Iron Age hill fort on Church Hill. There is, however, little hard evidence to support their case, although it would seem to be an ideal position for such a stronghold and its existence is not improbable. Others assert that as a place of antiquity, Church Hill was the site of a burgh, a fortified settlement, established in 916 by Aethelfleda, the wife of Aethelflaed, Lord of the Mercians. In her own right she was a powerful war leader against the Danes, especially after the death of her husband. She is brought to mind today in Ethelfleda Terrace on Church Hill, upon which it is thought that there are remains of earthworks that date back to the tenth century.

Again, there is not much evidence to back up this contention, although Church Hill would have been an excellent location for a burgh in the wars against the Danes. In fact the first documentary evidence for Wednesbury dates only to the Domesday Book of 1086 when it was given as Wadnesberie. That massive collection of material about Medieval England indicated that 28 men lived locally and that there was a mill of two shillings rent, one acre of meadow, and a wood two miles in length and one mile in breadth. That wood and others were to be crucial in making Wednesbury an industrial centre.

In the absence of archaeological findings and written sources, it is in its name that Wednesbury makes us hark to its place in the beginnings of England. It means Woden's fort and recalls the leading pagan god of the early Anglo-Saxons; as does nearby Wednesfield, which signifies the open ground of Woden and which was mentioned first in 996. Also remembered in Wednesday, Woden was regarded as the ancestor of the kings of the Mercians and was worshipped both in England and Germany, whilst he was called Odin by the Scandinavians.

The god war, of the dead, and of wisdom, Woden was the leader of the Wild Hunt, sweeping his pack of baying hounds across the stormy night sky. In this guise he became associated with Father Christmas, for Woden also raced across the night sky in his chariot to bear gifts

Wednesbury colliers about 1897 about to go down into the mine. Thanks to Ian Bott.

at the time of the winter solstice. Both Wednesbury and Wednesfield are rarities, for they are amongst just 20 existing place names in England that refer to the old gods of the Anglo Saxons. There must have been more, but as Christianity came to hold sway over kings, nobles and then the common people, it is likely that the Church encouraged the changing of such names.

In fact, it would seem that what is now the West Midlands was a bastion of pagan worship, as is made plain by other place names. Weeford, close to Tamworth and Lichfield, means the ford of the heathen temple – from the Anglo Saxon weoh, a heathen shrine or temple; Weoley Castle in Birmingham indicates a heathen shrine in a glade (leah); whilst Tyseley, also in Birmingham, may signify 'the sacred grove of Tiw', another Anglo-Saxon god remembered in the modern Tuesday.

Given this evidence, it would seem possible that there was a temple to Woden on the highest point in Wednesbury and that after the local people finally became Christians in the late 600s, a church was built on its site to make plain the dominance of Christianity over the old gods. Some historians argue that the stubborn devotion of the folk in and around Wednesbury to Woden and other pagan deities encouraged Saint Chad to make Lichfield the centre of the Mercian see. Located not far away, Lichfield acted both as a base for missionaries and as a nearby symbol of the power of Christianity.

After the Norman Conquest, the manor of Wednesbury belonged to the Crown, but in 1164 Henry II bestowed it upon the Heronvilles, best associated with Woodstock. They did not make themselves popular. In 1272, John Heronville was sued by 25 of his tenants. They claimed that he had exacted from them "other customs and services than they used to render when the manor was in the hands of the ancestors of the King".

Heronville was a lord who wanted his pound of flesh. He believed that his tenants ought to work for him for free for several days, to do his ploughing, mowing

Pit bonk wenches at the Blue Fly Colliery, Mesty Croft, Wednesbury, about 1897. Thanks to Ian Bott. Known by the better off as banks girls, these women did various jobs. Some took the tubs filled with coal as they came out of the mine and emptied them; others loaded coal on to the narrow boats on the cut; and yet more drove carts or shifted the ironstone from the shale. Their work was tough, long, dirty and low paid. They were looked down on by middle-class moralists for working at a 'man's job' and for their independent ways. In truth, they were hard-grafting women who had no choice but to do such a job if their families weren't to be clammed. Their distinctive inverted bonnets protected their hair.

and reaping. On top of that he wanted them to pay him taxes whenever he demanded them; he levied a penny on them to brew beer; he made them hand over 2 shillings (10p) to him when their children married; he forced them to pay him for the right to graze pigs on acorns and beech mast on the common land; and he demanded an 'inheritance tax' on half the worth of a deceased tenant's pigs, boar, male colts, cart bound with iron, uncut cloth, and whole hams.

Judgement was postponed for eight years and Heronville was ordered to give back to his tenants those goods in question. He did not do so. More than that, he interfered with their cultivation. Heronville was then prosecuted, but it is not known what was the outcome of the case. A generation or so later, in 1315, the extent of the family's landowning was made clear when Juliana Heronville, the widow of the lord of the manor, was recorded as owning 145 strips of arable land in the three great common fields: Monway Field, Church Field and Hall Field.

By this date, iron working and the gathering of coal was noticeable in Wednesbury, and miners appear as a distinct group locally by 1400. In his account of his journeying across England in the later 1530s and

The back-yard scene – Trow's Square, off Wednesbury Road, in 1933. This photograph is taken from a cracking new publication by Ian M. Bott, Wednesbury Memories (Sutton Publishing, £12.95). Ian has done a tremendous job in emphasising the history of Wednesbury and its people and he is one of a small but steadfast band of dedicated Black Country historians resolved to ensure that the past of various towns is brought forward into the present and the future. He has written a number of books on Wednesbury and like his previous publications, this one brings out of the shadows and into the glare of history a superb collection of photographs that bring life to the history of the town.

A bostin' photo of work to strengthen the banks of the River Tame at the new Crankhall Lane bridge in 1937. The contractor was Tarmac Ltd of Wolverhampton. The houses in view were later demolished. In the early days of the iron trade in Wednesbury, the Tame – although little more than a stream – was strong enough to power mills without the need to spend money on dams and pools.

early 1540s, John Leland noted that coal was found at Wednesbury and that Birmingham's smiths got their sea coal and much of their iron from Staffordshire, probably also from Wednesbury. In 1586, another notable traveller and writer, William Camden, wondered whether the coal mines and iron workings of Wednesbury would be a "commodity or hindrance of the inhabitants'". There is no doubt that they were a vital commodity.

To get at the coal in this period, workmen laboured in flat mines whereby they 'rid' off the earth and dug the coal from under their feet, carting it off in wheelbarrows. This procedure survived locally until the later seventeenth century, by which time it became necessary to sink deeper mines to gain access to the coal.

The Thick Coal of the South Staffordshire coalfield was liable to spontaneous combustion, and in 1680 it was reported that eleven acres of coal was smouldering below ground at Wednesbury. This was a longstanding problem, and in 1739 Dr Wilkes, a physician in Willenhall, wrote that broken or gob coal in the mines of the town "burns as long as the air can come to it, but goes out when it comes to a solid wall of coal. This evening, as I rode over part of the field where this fire was burning many acres together, the air being calm, and the weather being dry for about a fortnight, I saw on the surface of the ground, where the smoke issued out of the earth, as fine flowers of brimstone as could be made by art. They seemed to lie a handful or two in a place, but there was no possibility of going to them."

Over a century before this, Wednesbury had lost its woods and copses, felled as they were for the burning of charcoal, a product essential for the smelting of iron. With no local charcoal, iron was carried on pack horses to be smelted at Perry Barr and Aston. Despite this, an increasing number of Wednesbury people were involved in working iron. Prominent amongst them were nailers and smiths. Most were small-scale in their operations, but one Wednesbury man gained wealth and prestige from rising to become great iron master. He was John Jennens of Wednesbury Hall. When he died in 1653 he left an ironworks, 100 loads of charcoal, 30 tons of pig iron and mines.

Interestingly, Wednesbury was also noted for its pottery, known as Wedgebury ware after the dialect name for the town. In his *Natural History of Staffordshire* (1686), Robert Plot recorded that there were two main centres of pottery production in Staffordshire – with the one in the north around Burslem

Market day on August 11 1968. Wednesbury's market is long-established. Originally held on a Friday, it was praised in the early nineteenth century as "well supplied with provisions of every description, and is numerously attended both by sellers and buyers, from the populous surrounding parishes". The town also boasted two annual cattle fairs held on May 6 and August 3, and a wake, or feast, which began on the Sunday nearest to St Bartholomew's Day.

being bigger than the other in the south. He mentioned that at Wednesbury "divers sorts of vessels' were made and painted with a reddish kind of slip from "earth gotten at Tipton".

It is apparent that the making of pottery was long-established, for in the recent archaeological digs in Birmingham's Bull Ring, a variety of pottery from Wednesbury dating from in later Middle Ages has been found, and by the seventeenth century the town was supplying the people of Birmingham with most of their everyday pottery. The Wednesbury potters continued to work throughout the eighteenth century, but about 1800 they closed down their works and migrated to the Pottery district of North Staffordshire. By then Wednesbury was beginning to gain fame for its metal work and as a centre of Methodism.

Chapter 9

PREACHING AT THE HORSE BLOCK IN WEDNESBURY: JOHN WESLEY

For such a peaceful and holy person who preached that each man and woman should love thy neighbour, John Wesley aroused terrible anger and violence against himself. Converted in 1738 within days of his brother, Charles, and after feeling his "heart strangely warmed", John Wesley truly trusted in Christ and set himself the thankless task of reaching out to all those damned by the rest of society as reprobates and unworthy of salvation. Wesley believed passionately that even the most dissolute person could be saved from a life of sin and turned to the way of the Lord. And perhaps therein lay the reason why he was so vilified and attacked: for in holding out the hand of brotherhood to drunkards, gamblers, fighters, the poor and the excluded, he challenged the smugness of a religious establishment that had become comfortable with its own self-righteousness.

A preacher within the Church of England, yet was Wesley subjected to the scorn and hatred of some Anglican ministers. As he traipsed across England, drawing to him great crowds to hear his words of Christian love at open-air meetings, that loathing led a minority of ordained priests to stir up the local mob. One such place was at Wednesbury. Charles Wesley had visited there during 1742, preaching nearby at Holloway Bank, Hill Top in West Bromwich. Now a housing estate, then this was a big natural hollow which could hold several thousand people. Charles was encouraged by his reception and asked his brother to follow him to Wednesbury. This John did in January 1743. It was to be the first of 33 visits to the Black Country town - his last coming on 22 March 1790, when he was 87.

Arriving on horseback on that first visit, Wesley rested and spoke that evening in the old Town Hall in Wednesbury's market place. He preached there again on the Sunday and later that day addressed a large gathering of folk in 'The Hollow'. After that first trip to Wednesbury about 100 folk locally were stirred to join Wesley's religious society, and soon their numbers grew three and four fold. At first, Reverend Egginton, the local Vicar, proved friendly to the emerging Methodists, telling Wesley that the oftener he came the better he should be pleased. But within weeks, relations became soured after one of Wesley's local preachers had "abused" the clergy. Egginton was transformed into an implacable enemy of the new

The Market Cross in Wednesbury, which stood there from 1709 to 1824. The butter market was held below and the room above was used as a town hall. Wesley preached there. This is from a drawing by F. C. Proctor and is taken from H. H. Prince, West Bromwich , or, the Story of Long Ago (West Bromwich, 1924).

movement. In April Wesley came to Wednesbury again and declared that Egginton preached so "wicked a Sermon", the like of which he had never heard; whilst a drunken clergyman tried to ride down some of the congregation at one of Wesley's meetings.

A month later, Charles Wesley met with "our dear colliers at Wednesbury and consecrated a piece of ground given for a preaching-place by singing a hymn upon it"; but when he preached from the steps of the market house at Walsall, a throng roared and threw stones at him. Then in June, rioters attacked Methodists in Wednesbury, bruising them and smashing their windows and furniture. The persecuted people appealed to the magistrates for protection, but were told that they were to blame for the outrages against them. Wesley was certain that the assaults had been kindled by local clergymen who had been inciting them through their sermons. Determinedly, he made his way to Wednesbury to help.

After he left trouble continued to brew and boiled over when John Wesley returned to Wednesbury on 20 October. He "preached in a ground near the middle of the town, to a far larger congregation than was expected". That afternoon, the cry arouse that the mob was besetting the house of Francis Ward, where Wesley was staying. Thankfully the unruly crowd dispersed, but unhappily returned at five in the afternoon. As if they were one enraged person, the mob called, "Bring out the minister; we will have the minister."

Courageous as ever, Wesley requested their leader to come into the house, and as he recalled in his journal, "after a few sentences interchanged between us, the lion became a lamb. I desired him to go and bring one or two more of the most angry of his companions. He brought in two who were ready to swallow the ground with rage; but in two minutes they were as calm as he. I then bade them make way that I might go out among the people."

Wesley asked them what they were after. They replied that they wanted him to go to the justices with them. He agreed readily and spoke a few inspired words, "so that they cried out, with might and main, 'The gentleman is an honest gentleman, and we will spill our blood in his defence.'" In the dark and the rain, Wesley went with the throng of two or three hundred to the house of Mr Lane at Bentley Hall. The crowd was told to take Wesley back. Then one of them informed Lane's son of the reason why the Methodists had aroused their ire: "Why, an't please you, they sing psalms all day; nay, and make folks rise at five in the morning. And what would your worship advise us to do?" Once again the angry pack was instructed to go home.

Wednesbury Bridge, in 1890. The bridge was built in 1821 and later widened. In the centre are houses painted white, and to the left of these is the house of Francis Ward, from which Wesley was dragged in 1743.

Undeterred, they decided to take Wesley to Walsall to another justice, who refused to rise from his bed. At last it was agreed that about 50 folk of the Darlaston mob would escort Wesley back to Wednesbury. Unfortunately, as they made their way "the mob of Walsall came, pouring in like a flood, and bore down all before them". The leader of the Darlaston people was a woman. She had sworn that no-one would touch Wesley and when "she saw her followers give way, ran into the thickest of the throng and knocked down three or four men, one after another".

Assaulted by many, the brave woman was overpowered and was kept down and beaten by three men who probably would have killed her. Then a man shouted out, "'Hold, Tom, hold!' 'Who is there?' said Tom: 'What, honest Munchin? Nay, then, let her go.'" So as Wesley recounted, the men let her get up and crawl home as well as she could.

Wesley was dragged to Walsall by his captors, amid the cries of some to kill him. So great was the clamour of the mob that it was like the roaring of the sea. Feeling no pain or weariness, the undaunted preacher eventually persuaded the crowd to listen to him, asking them "What evil have I done? Which of you all have I wronged in word or deed?" But after fifteen minutes his voice suddenly failed and "then the floods began to lift up their voice again; many crying out, 'Bring him away! Bring him away!'"

Grasping hardily on to his faith, Wesley refound his voice and strength and broke out aloud in prayer. The man who had led the mob was converted on the spot, exclaiming "Sir, I will spend my life for you: follow me, and not one soul here shall touch a hair of your head." It was the same Munchin as had saved the female leader of the Darlaston mob. Munchin and two or three companions protected Wesley, whilst the shopkeeper of the premises by which he had stopped cried shame on the rabble. An honest butcher pulled back four or five of the ruffians "who were running on the most fiercely. The people then, as if it had been by common consent, fell back to the right and left, while those three or four men took me between them and carried me through them all. But on the bridge the mob rallied again: we therefore went on one side, over the milldam, and thence through the meadows; till, a little before ten, God brought me safe to Wednesbury; I having lost only one flap of my waistcoat and a little skin from one of my hands."

Later, Wesley brought to mind the remarkable way he had been saved from a vicious beating or death. If he had slipped at any time he would not have risen. None of the mob was able to catch hold properly of his collar or clothes. Somehow a "lusty" man's blows against him with a large oaken stick were turned aside from the back of his head. One man who went to hit him dropped his hand "and only stroked my head, saying, 'What soft hair he has.'" When Wesley stopped to speak out in Walsall, he did so at the spot where the mayor was standing in his shop door, so that his presence was "the first check to the madness of the people".

The "very first men whose hearts were turned were the heroes of the town, the captains of the rabble on all occasions, one of them having been a prizefighter at the bear-garden". From first to last, no-one reviled Wesley or insulted him, instead he was called "the preacher", "the parson", or "the minister". Importantly, none of the mob had a charge to put against Wesley. And finally, "they were as utterly at a loss what they should do with me, none proposing any determinate thing only 'Away with him! Kill him at once!'"

Nor did Wesley forget a valiant foursome of local Methodists who stayed with him when their fellows fled after Wesley was hauled from Wednesbury. They were William Sitch, Edward Slater, John Griffiths, and Joan Parks. As Wesley wrote with admiration, "these kept with me, resolving to live or die together; and none of them received one blow but William Sitch, who held me by the arm from one end of the town to the other. He was then dragged away and knocked down; but he soon rose and got to me again. I afterward asked him what he expected when the mob came upon us. He said, 'To die for Him who had died for us': and he felt no hurry or fear but calmly waited till God should require his soul of him."

Joan Parks was also torn from Wesley's side, but averred that she was no more afraid "than I am now. I could trust God for you, as well as for myself. From the beginning I had a full persuasion that God would deliver you. I knew not how; but I left that to Him, and was as sure as if it were already done."

Back at the home of Francis Ward many people unconnected with the Methodists came to show Wesley their support and the next morning, "as I rode through the town in my way to Nottingham,

The cross indicates a cottage off Bridge Street, once the home of "Honest Munchin," a converted ruffian who rescued John Wesley from his would-be murderers in the historic Wednesbury riots in 1743. He died at Birmingham in 1789, at the age of 85, and his tombstone may be seen in St. Paul's Churchyard there.

Honest Munchin's cottage about 1890, at the rear of the Fountain Inn, Holloway Bank, Wednesbury. It was demolished in 1934. Thanks to Ian Bott.

Wesley in the hands of the mob at Wednesbury, taken from a painting by Marshall Claxton RA.

everyone I met expressed such a cordial affection that I could scarcely believe what I saw and heard".

In a blatant piece of unjustness, the local magistrates blamed Methodist preachers for raising "routs and riots, to the great damage of his Majesty's liege people, and against the peace of our Sovereign Lord the King", and ordered a diligent search for said Methodist preachers. But such actions failed to hold back the growing number of conversions to Methodism. Prominent amongst the new believers was Honest Munchin, the erstwhile leader of the mob. Damned previously as the "greatest profligate of the country", in the spirit of John Wesley's preaching, Munchin had saved his brother.

Five days after the riot, Charles Wesley admitted Munchin on trial into the Methodist Society. Charles asked what he thought of his brother. "Think of him? That he is a man of God; and God was on his side, when so many of us could not kill one man." Munchin's real name was George Clifton and he was from West Bromwich. He died in Birmingham aged eighty-five in 1789, two years before Wesley, and he never wearied of telling the story of the night when God saved him from laying his hand on His servant.

Never again did Wesley suffer at the hands of the mob in the Black Country. Indeed, the Black Country was to become one of the centres of working-class Methodism – along with Cornwall, where Wesley also suffered grievously. Much of Wesley's preaching in Wednesbury was done from the horse block situated in High Bullen near where the first meeting house was built. This block is now inside the

Central Church, Spring Head, whilst a plaque on Church Hill commemorates the open-air preaching spot. The Central Church at Spring Head also keeps the Dingley Collection. Dr Edward Dingley (1860-1948) was a highly-respected doctor in Wednesbury GP and gathered many items relating to John and Charles Wesley. Amongst his collection are a piece of cast iron thrown at Wesley during the 1743-44 riots, various items of sculpture, a Breeches Bible and Francis Ward's Bible in which it was recorded that John Wesley baptised his children.

The horse block in Wednesbury from which Wesley preached.

Wedgebury Cocking

At Wednesbury there was a cocking,
A match between Newton and Scroggins.
The Colliers and Nailors left work,
And all to old Spittle's went jogging.
To see this noble sport, me lads,
Many noble men resorted.
And though they'd little of money, me lads,
With that they freely sported.

Chorus: "Oh, it's off to the fight," cried Bill Cartwright,
    "And it's off to the fight," cried he.
    "Oh, it's off to the fight," cried Bill Cartwright,
    "And it's off to the fight," cried he.

There was Jeffory and Oldborn from Hampton
And Dusty from Bilston was there.
Plummery, he came from Darlaston,
And he was as rude as a bear.
Old Will, he came from Walsall, me lads,

And Smacker from West Brom. come.
Blind Robin, he came from Rowley, me lads,
And staggering, he went whum.

Ralph Moody come hobbling along,
As though he some cripple was mocking,
To join in the blackguard throng,
That met at Wednesbury Cocking.
He borrowed a trifle of Doll, me lads,
To back old Taverner's grey.
He laid fourpence half-penny to fourpence, me lads,
Then lost and went broken away.

But soon he returned to the pit,
For he'd borrowed a trifle of money,
And ventured another large bet,
Along with blobber-mouth Coney.
Then Coney demanded his money, me lads,
Which is common on all such occasions.
He cried, "Blast thee if thee don't bold thy peace, me lads.
I'll pay thee as Paul paid the Ephesians."

Then they all returned to the pit,
And the fighting went forward again.
Six battles were fought on each side,
And the next to decide the main.
For they were two famous cocks, me lads,
As ever this country bred,
Scroggins' a duck-winged black, me lads,
And Newton's a shift-wing red.

The conflict was hard on both sides,
Till brassy-winged black's was choked.
The colliers were nationally vexed,
And the nailors were sorely provoked.
Peter Stephens, he swore a great oath, me lads,
That Scroggins had played his cock foul.
Scroggins, he gave him a kick, me lads,
And cried, "God damn your soul."

The company then fell in a discord,
A bold fight did ensue.
Kick b . . . and bite was the word,
Till the Walsall men were subdued.
Ralph Moody bit off a man's nose, me lads,
And wished that he could have him slain,
So they trampled him to death me lads,
And they made a draw of the main.

The cockpit was near to the church,
An ornament unto the town.
On one side was an old coal pit,
The other well gorsed around.
Peter Hadley peeped through the gorse, me lads,
In order to see them fight.
Spittle jobbed his eye out with a fork, me lads,
And said, "Blast thee! It serves thee right."

Some people may think this is strange,
Who Wednesbury never knew,
But those who have ever been there
Won't have the least doubt but it's true.
For they are savage by nature, me lads,
And guilty of deeds most shocking,
Jack Baker he whacked his own father, me lads,
And so ended Wednesbury cocking.

This well-known song (which has more verses) was popular on broadsheets from the early nineteenth century and it played upon the hard reputation that Wednesbury had for fighting men and cockfighting. According to some stories, when the old stage coach used to pass through the town, one of the guards would blow the tune of the 'Wedgebury Cocking'. Another old song, 'The Wedgefield Wake', also recounts how a large gathering of cockfighters at Wednesfield finished up in a mass brawl, after the champion cock of Wedgefield showed signs of defeat against the champion cock of the Willenhall lads. On this occasion, the Wedgefield chaps joined in with those from Wednesfield. Interestingly, Saint Bartholomew's, the parish church of Wednesbury, has a most unusual feature: a wooden lectern dating from the fourteenth century that is in the form of a fighting cock instead of the usual eagle.

Chapter 10

FANNING THE FIRE: BILSTON METHODISM

Wednesbury and Walsall were not the only places in the Black Country visited by John Wesley. Bilston was also honoured by his preaching. The first recorded visit of John Wesley locally was on 9 November 1745. The founder of Methodism wrote in his journal that "it was exceedingly dark when we rode through Bilstone. However, we did not stick fast until we came to Wednesbury town end. Several coming with candles, I got out of the quagmire; and leaving them to disengage my horse, walked to Francis Ward's and preached from: Fear not ye, for I know that ye seek Him that was crucified".

It was Harold Dale of Bilston who kindly alerted me to the relationship between his own noteworthy Black Country town and the great preacher. The details are taken from an important book by Harold's wife, Iris, which recounts the sturdy history of Bilston Methodism and I thank Iris for sharing them with me. Iris indicates that Iris reveals that Wesley would have travelled from Penkridge to Wolverhampton and entered Bilston via Wolverhampton Street – then known as Shift End. Riding down High Street and Church Street, across Swan Bank he would have turned down Bridge Street (then called 'The Old Road'), then crossed the brook on the north side of Saint Mary's Church and followed the Old Road, curving towards Darlaston which would have led him into Dangerfield Lane and so on to Wednesbury where his horse "stuck fast".

At the time of Wesley's first visit, Iris points out that Bilston was a small place with population of only around 3,000. It was still embedded in a rural setting, with several farm houses within the town itself and many people employed on the local farms. Others worked in the mines or quarries or made glass, pottery, buckles or locks. Apparently there was only one place of worship, the parish church of St Leonard – the origins of which dated to the tenth century.

Shortly after Wesley left, several houses were opened up for Methodist meetings. Two early converts were Stephen Hipkiss, a miner, and Samuel Ferriday, whose old half-timbered house was situated in Market Street opposite the Pype Hall. A frequent visitor to this house was John Wesley's friend, Francis Ward of Wednesbury, who helped to "fan the Methodist fire" in Bilston. Meetings were also held in Peggy Taylor's home in 'Hangman's Row' (later Warwick Street) and in that of Mr. Homer, the enameller of Homer's Fold.

John Wesley subsequently visited the town on a number of occasions, especially in 1767 and 1768 when he was himself a minister in the Staffordshire Circuit, to which Bilston belonged. As elsewhere in the Black Country, Wesley was badly treated by mobs, often stirred up by Anglican churchmen and establishment figures. One morning in 1770 while the Bilston Methodists were holding a meeting in Samuel Ferriday's house a crowd of drunkards gathered in the street and began to shout and to sing in order to drown the sound of the hymns. They threw stones at the windows and two of John Wesley's friends were injured.

Again and again the mob bayed out for "the preacher". Calm as ever he was in violent and threatening situations, Wesley appeared at the door. A hefty man who was a bull-baiter stepped forward with an uplifted stick as if to hit the preacher. Wesley looked at the enraged chap and said quite calmly, "If I have done thee any harm, strike man." Like a lion turned into a lamb, the bull baiter lowered his arm. So powerful were Wesley's demeanour and composure that the bull-baiter became the champion of the founder of Methodism. Ass for the rest of the ruffians, according to tradition they were so impressed that they immediately became followers of Wesley.

During the next twenty years Methodism in Bilston grew slowly but steadily. The little society was well organised with its own local preachers, class leaders and stewards, many of whose names are now lost. They must have been a hardy yet spiritual bunch for John Freeman wrote of them that "you feel at once that they had touched some Eternal reality". These early Bilston Methodists suffered much from the antagonism of Anglicans in the town and from the local clergy. Rejected they may have been but still they refused to be marginalised and to foreswear their faith.

A poor congregation, the Methodists could not afford to build a chapel for worship and for many years they worshipped in each other's homes and in the open air. One of these pioneering Methodists was Peggy Taylor. She was praised as a woman "who was too poor to buy sugar but she was uncommonly strong in faith and humour, two qualities always essential in a pioneer". She worked closely with Miss Anne Loxdale, the second daughter of Thomas and Hannah Loxdale. Anne had been christened in Shrewsbury on 1 October 1755 and the family later moved to Bilston. She had been converted by John Wesley himself while still young, although her parents and relations, who were wealthy and devout Anglicans, all declared that she was mad.

These two very different ladies worked closely together. With others they met at Peggy's house for a cup of tea to plan how to provide a Meeting House. At that time tea cost 8/- a pound and sugar almost as much. Peggy confessed she had no sugar but offered her guests a lump of "penny an ounce" from the bottles of sweets that she sold from her front window. In 1794 Miss Loxdale gave a piece of land in Temple Street to the society on which to build a chapel. For many years this was known as 'Loxdale's chapel'. It was built with bricks taken from an old demolished engine house. A gallery was built to seat the choir for the tradition that "Methodism was born in song" was very true with the first Bilston Methodists.

The day of the opening of the chapel was a momentous one for Bilston, as Iris stresses. The opening sermon was preached by the Reverend Joseph Benson, the Methodist scholar and commentator. Mrs Fanny Brooke was converted at this service and in 1797 she founded the town's first Sunday School – and one of the oldest in Methodism - in the kitchen of her home in Church Street. She began with two small girls and her seven year old son James, who later became a Methodist minister. The next week several other children arrived. They were taught to write and to read the Bible and how to pray. Soon there were too many children to meet in Mrs Brookes's house and with help of friends she moved the Sunday School into the Methodist chapel in Temple Street, Bilston.

John Freeman described the chapel itself as "a small building with an open roof, supported by plain cross-beams. At the entrance end was a gallery with no front protection, which led to the whimsical sight of men sitting on the gallery floor while their legs dangled over the lower congregation. The simplicity of construction was emphasised by the fact that access to the gallery was gained by an ordinary ladder; The Circuit Ministers always travelled in the saddle, and accommodation had to be found for the shelter and feeding of their horses. This was done by partitioning off with boards a space in the Chapel; and it was quite usual for the sermon and prayers to be punctuated by the tinkle of a chain, and other stable noises."

One of the dedication services at the chapel was taken by Dr.

Artist's impression of

Loxdale's Temple Street Chapel

The First known Methodist Chapel in Bilston

After the improvements of 1812

An artist's impression of the first Methodist chapel in Temple Street Bilston.

Thomas Coke, who was a clergyman of the Church of England, as indeed were John and Charles Wesley themselves. Coke had visited America on several occasions and had worked with Francis Asbury, who was born in Great Barr and whose impact on North American Methodism was profound. On one of these journeys there were very rough seas and they were at sea for 13 weeks. In a very severe storm the ship had to shelter in the West Indies. On Christmas day 1786 Dr. Coke landed in Antigua with three young missionaries. He preached to two thousand Black people who were enslaved and because of this the Wesleyan Foreign Missionary Society was founded. It later became known as the Methodist Missionary Society.

The 1823 Chapel on the Swan Bank site.

At Bilston, Coke preached on winning the world for Christ and found in Miss Loxdale a kindred spirit for missionary work. He paid many more visits to Bilston and ultimately married Anne Loxdale in 1811. Their zeal for missionary work grew but sadly Anne died shortly before their first wedding anniversary.

Although the Methodists now had their own chapel they did not administer their own sacraments. The Bilston Methodists attended the parish church for communion but some of them were refused permission to take communion at St. Leonard's and had to walk two or three miles to Wednesbury or Darlaston to receive the host.

The Methodist Society of Bilston was growing markedly and the little chapel in Temple Street was always filled. Sometimes folk had to be turned away from the public services. Prayer meetings, class meetings and other activities took place regularly. By 1812 more accommodation was pressingly needed and it was decided to provide seventy more seats in the chapel by inserting side galleries and a special pew for singers.

A stirring revival had taken place in the locality in 1815 led by a lay preacher called Spink and this had led to a further growth in the society. Consequently in 1822 it was decided to build another chapel in Brook Street, although there was much opposition to this plan. Some bricks had already been laid when the owner of the land discovered that his agents had agreed to sell to Methodists and immediately he withdrew the sale. At last in 1823, and despite many problems, a new and bigger chapel was opened for worship at Swan Bank. It was built on land sold by the Loxdale family. This chapel was the first building in Bilston to be lit by gas and because of its success it was enlarged in 1840 and again in 1890 so that it could accommodate 1,000 worshippers.

Better known as Bilston Wesley the chapel gained a fine reputation for its music festivals, its award-winning choirs and its Binn's pipe organ. In 1955, the Wesleyan and Primitive Methodist Circuits amalgamated, followed eight years later by a coming together of the Wesley and the High Street Methodist Church at the Swan Bank chapel. Thus was formed the Bilston Methodist Church. The old chapel was knocked down in 1969 and replaced a year later by a new place of worship on the same site. Almost two and hundred and sixty

The 1840 Chapel or enlargement. This site is where the 1832 mass cholera burial was.

years on from Wesley's first visit to Bilston, local Methodists continue to preach his message of goodwill and salvation to all men and women.

The Story of Bilston Wesley by Iris Dale looks at the period between 1823 and 1963. It is available from Harold and Iris or from Bilston Methodist Church at a cost of £5.00, postage extra. I pay tribute to the research of Iris and the way in which she has brought out of the shadows of the past people like Peggy Taylor, a woman who despite her hardships was prepared to share what she had with others in accordance with her Christian beliefs.

1890 modifications of the chapel with the manse.

Chapter 11

ARTISTS IN THE SAND: CRADLEY CASTINGS

Reading the articles on the chainmakers of the Black Country encouraged Bev Pegg, now of Hagley, to send me a copy of a book on his family firm, Cradley Castings Limited. Called *Through the Years*, it alerts us to the importance of the multitude of small and medium-sized metal fashioning companies to the emergence of the Black Country as one of the greatest manufacturing regions the world has known. Crucially, the closure of the business in 2002 highlights the problems adversely affecting all those firms engaged in the making of things. Faced with losing turnover to Eastern European and Far Eastern concerns, the Peggs had no choice but to pack up after a distinguished history. The loss of such an enterprise emphasises not only the difficulties of competing with cheap labour economies but also of how our national politicians of all types have failed miserably to recognise the importance of manufacturing both to the economic and social well being of the nation.

Bev traces his involvement in the metal industries to his grandparents. Phoebe Worton was a chainmaker who worked in her family's chain shop, believed to have been in the Beecher Road locality of Colley Gate, Cradley. In 1907 she married William Pegg and they went on to live Alma Street, Colley Gate. Fourteen years later William joined two other local chaps to set up The Cradley Chain and manufacturing Company. His partners were John 'Jack' Ness of Old Hill and Harry Forrest of Chapel Street, Colley Gate, who was married to William's younger sister, Minnie.

Together they focused upon making small chain up to about 1 inch in a workshop at the bottom end of Mill Street, which ran parallel with the River Stour. Jack was a life-long pal of William's and was recalled as "a big, strong man of gentle disposition" who was a tireless, hard worker. Sadly he died in 1938 whilst in his early forties. Harry stayed with the business for six years, leaving it in October 1927 when it became a limited company.

By this time, competition from machine-made chain was beginning to hit hard the hand-made chainmakers, especially in the lighter end of the trade. Still, William soldiered on, but matters changed drastically in 1945 when his son Ashley became a shareholder. Trading was bad, so much so that Ashley tried to sell the business at a knock-down price of £450. There were no takers. Two options remained: either close up shop or move into new products. Determined to make things work, Ashley decided to try his hand at iron castings and so shifted into the foundry trade. The first thing to do was to put in a small cupola, a furnace for melting metals. As

Chainmakers outside the Worton family chain shop about 1902. Phoebe Worton, who later married William Pegg, is on the right.

All the photos in this article are courtesy of Bev Pegg. Both Ashley Pegg and his wife, Norah, were well-known singers. Ashley appeared regularly on the radio and sang for a number of various operatic societies, whilst Norah won the National Caroll Levis Discovery of the year title and was accepted by the Royal Opera House, Covent Garden. A fine soprano, she also made numerous broadcasts. Bev Pegg himself is a well-known singer. Bev himself is noted singer and has kindly given me a copy of his LP, 'The Foundry Ditty and the Industrial Air'. He thinks "it is the only album ever dedicated to the foundry industry. In fact I know it is. Who else would be daft enough to do such a thing." It is a cracking album, and in one song Bev admiringly calls moulders "artists in the sand". Bev intends to bring it out as a CD. Further details will be available on his web site www.bevpegg.co.uk

I also thank Harry Rowlands for scanning and sending me the photos that I have used.

important was the need to take on capable hand moulders and a foreman who knew what he was about – and Wilf Edge was that man. Then the new operation had to have a knowledgeable works manager, who was found in Ken Newton.

Initially, the company sub-contracted work for bigger foundries, one of which was William Whitehouse Limited of the Stourbridge Road in Halesowen. The general manager there was Ernie Hudson, a good friend of Ashley Pegg, who was ever-ready to help out with advice. About 1951, Ernie recommended to Ashley that he take on one of his blokes, Les Breakwell, as foundry manager. Les was alert to the improvements that were needed to move Cradley Chain forward and he grasped the opportunity handed to him.

Trade was up and down, but still the foundry side of the business grew and as it did so the chainmaking petered out, although as late as 1952 a number of chainmakers remained active. Amongst them was Clarrie Johnson. When the Black Country Living Museum was opened, Clarrie was one of the first people to demonstrate chainmaking there. By now, the firm was also producing grey iron castings. A crystalline metal, cast iron is an iron alloy that contains carbon and is produced in a blast furnace – a substantial brick or stone structure, the interior of which looked like two cones or pyramids placed base to base. Great bellows forced air into the heart of the furnace where a roaring fire melted the raw material that had been fed into the top. The molten iron was then let out into open moulds of a pig bed. This was so called because it was said to resemble pigs feeding from a sow.

Once cooled, the pig iron could then be taken to furnaces where it was melted down and cast. This cast iron cannot be forged, rolled or welded whether it is hot or cold, but it is ideal for pouring when molten into moulds, the shape of which it takes when it cools. In the nineteenth century cast iron was widely used for making household utensils, cannon, small arms, building frames, water and sewer pipes, and bridges. In fact the Iron Bridge at Coalbrookdale that brought fame to Abraham Darby III was built in 1779 from iron castings.

In the 1950s at Cradley Chain, the moulders would line up at the furnace spout to wait their turn for the molten metal to be poured into their moulding ladles – sometimes known as pots. From there they would walk into one of the moulding sections where they cast their moulds. Each mould was made of sand within which was a core made from sand and oil that had been baked in an oven to become hard like a biscuit. This core gave the internal shape and would not come apart when the metal flowed into it.

Once the casting had cooled, the core was banged away with a hammer. Bev Pegg recalled that "the standard moulding sizes at that time were 25" x 20" x 16", which catered for the emphasis in production of slide rails, trivets, top plates and burners for the gas and electric cooker trade. Shafts of light cut through the smoke and fumes during the metal pouring time of the day."

A group of chainmakers in 1952. Left to right are Bill Kendrick, Cliff Guest, Will Pegg, Clarrie Johnson, David Powell, Hartley Clifton, unknown, Ivan Penn and Jack Roberts.

With Health and Safety regulations at a minimum, there was no protective footwear and one occasion there was an accident involving one of the moulders, Jack Smith. Unfortunately, he had poured some of the boiling hot metal over his foot and not into his mould, burning away much of the foot. The pain must have been excruciating for the cast iron was 1500 degrees centigrade hot. Bev sped with the injured worker to Birmingham Accident Hospital. Smelling the burning flesh he asked Jack, "How does it feel?" The reply was typical of a phlegmatic and understated Black Country man, for all Jack said was, "It's a bit warm."

By now, there were two cupolas that could be seen from the Lyde Green entrance of the works and which were covered in a structure made of corrugated sheets so as to contain emissions. Mill Street itself had been half taken over by Cradley Chain and the company continued to move its main gates further and further up the street as it bought more houses and integrated them into the works. The last person to live in the street was Albert Lowe, who was featured in the

Express and Star in 1963. He was offered a modern council property nearby, but his answer was firm: "The only way I'll leave here is when they me out in a box". With his house within the gates of what was now called Cradley Chain and Castings Ltd, Albert was given keys so he could get in and out and lived his life amidst the moulding shops and cupolas.

His son, Harold, joined the company in 1946 and became works caretaker. From his home at 33, Mill Street he and his family moved to the 'Bridge Inn' on Bridge Street, across the way from Mill Street. This had been bought by the firm in 1954 and for a short while it was used as offices. Two years later, however, the offices were moved back into Mill Street so as to be closer to the works. The old pub remained home to Harold and his family until it was cleared by the Council in 1969 for road widening and the building of flats. He then moved to a house owned by Cradley Chain and Castings in Lyde Green. Harold was remembered as a loyal employee who worked on until just before he died in 1991.

Like his fellow workers, Harold, was a regular on works outings and doos, for as with so many industrial businesses, Cradley Chain and Castings was more than

Charlie Cole, Jack Brooks and others casting moulds 1953.

a place of work, it was also a social centre. Trips were organised to Blackpool, Christmas dinners were put on each year at the Old Hill Civic Hall, and there was a works football side. In the 1970/71 season, this team won the Birmingham AFA Premier League Championship, a tremendous achievement for a small works at a time when there were scores upon scores of works football teams in the Black Country and Brummagem. Winning their last fifteen games to take the title by a clear margin of six points, the side lost out on the double in the final of the AFA Senior Cup. Three years later, Cradley Castings Football team again won the league, and in the seven years from 1967 it always finished in the top three.

With the castings business growing, the decision was taken to convert the old chain shop, but on 19 January 1960 an accident befell the men carrying out the job. Walter Hackett of Kinver was inside the building when its 30 foot high wall began sagging inwards. Hearing a rumbling he ran for it, not realising that Peter Westwood, a steel erector of Amblecote who had been measuring up, was left behind to be buried after the roof caved in and the building collapsed. Other workers rushed to the aid of their mate, pulling from him the bricks and ironwork that had covered him. Peter was rushed to hospital with head and suspected internal injuries. It seems that the collapse had been caused by water lying behind a bank of earth behind the wall.

Reg Cole and Wally Smith pouring their moulds on traditional floor moulding lines.

Moulders queuing for metal at the furnace spout in 1953. Left to right are Fred Homer, Alf Kirton, Danny Moore, Jesse Penn, Tommy Priest, Billy Hill and Roy Woodhouse.

Growing in confidence in its ability to produce castings, the firm moved into the more high quality market with castings for diesel engines, pumps, compressors, machine tools and general engineering. Having been with the company for a number of years, Les Breakwell moved on to become a director at The Bank Hardware Company, which became a competitor to Cradley Chain and Castings. Fortunately, Bev Pegg was able to take up a position as managing director. Grandson of the founder, he had worked both in the foundry and pattern shop and had attended technical school.

The following years saw further expansion. In 1965, the company bought the Phoenix Works of The Sheet Iron Workers Ltd, which had just gone into liquidation. Five years later these premises, also in Mill Street, were demolished and replaced with a new warehouse, whilst in 1972 the company became Cradley Castings Limited. This signified the end of the link with chainmaking. Indeed, the last chains made in house left the works in 1957, "although Ashley Pegg personally attended to supplying some of his longstanding good customers with their chain needs right up to the late 1960s".

The change in name was accompanied by technological progress. Until 1972 manual bench and floor moulding dominated the company's output, but then it was

The retirement of Fred Williams 3 May 1996. Fred started work for the company in February 1952. Left to right are Yvonne Cox, Barry Pardoe, Ann Felton, Ernie Wilkinson, Bev Pegg, Malcolm Stringer, Terry Jeavons, Lew Bloomer, Trevor Willetts, Harry Homer, Fred Williams, David Quarry, Barry Phipps, Alan Pearson, Alan Yates, Mick McHale, Mohammed Riaz, and Malcolm Beardsmore.

decided to bring in a mechanised moulding line that would increase production, give a more a consistent standard of casting, and partly alleviate the problem caused by the difficulty in finding workers skilled enough in the traditional method of green sand moulding. To achieve these objectives, an American 'Newago' snap flask moulding system was bought. Installed in 1973 by Bright Grayson, photographs were taken of it on site to provide an advertisement in the *Foundry Trade Journal*.

With output up and factory legislation increasing, Alan Yates was brought in as general manager in 1977. Alan was highly experienced. He had served his apprenticeship in the foundry trade with Birmid Industries and had gone on to become principal investigations officer at the British Cast Iron Research Association, advising Cradley Castings on investment in new plant and systems. After the death of Ashley Pegg in 1982, Alan became managing director and Bev Pegg took over as chairman.

Awarded a BS 5750 certification in 1991, Cradley Castings celebrated its 75th anniversary with a party at the 'Rose and Crown' in Cradley on 5 April 1996 and at which the star guest was Tommy Mundon. With a workforce of 54 people, Cradley Castings produced grey iron castings to BS 1452 1990 Grades 220 and 250. Production ranged from 'one-offs' to batches of 2,500, whilst the individual casting weight ranged from 250 grams to 100 kilograms.

On a separate building on the site, there was an aluminium sand casting foundry also operating to British Standards. Although most moulding was machined, Cradley Castings still employed craftsmen who used bench and floor moulds and who were skilled at loose pattern work. The metal itself was melted in two cold blast cupolas, whilst a self-contained core shop provided cores to the iron foundry. Quality control was administered by a sophisticated Dewtec computer system.

Committed to supplying top quality goods to exact specification and delivered when promised, Cradley Casting weathered the recession of the 1980s that felled so many of our metal based companies. Reaching the new millennium, it was no longer able to compete in a world market where big businesses are forcing down prices to cut-throat margins. In another nation, politicians would have been looking for ways to back firms like Cradley Castings, firms that had embraced technology and that have added value. But in a Britain that unwisely shrinks from manufacturing as something outdated in a mature economy and which foolishly does not give status to engineering, then there was no likelihood of that happening. Will it only be when we make nothing that we realise how important it is to make things?

Chapter 12

FARMS, CHEMICALS AND METALS AT THE LONG CLEARING: LANGLEY

As cars rush up and down the Birmingham New Road, many motorists still look out for the landmark of the old 'Hen and Chickens' pub at Langley. For most of them, this is as close as they will ever come to Langley – and more's the pity, for it is one of those distinctive, Black Country places that boasts a thriving village centre with specialist, independent retailers offering fine service and good value and cracking festivities for the switching on of its Christmas light. And that vital heart to Langley is not just the result of chance, it has come to life because of the history of this area.

An Anglo-Saxon place name, Langley means the long (lang) wood or clearing. Its name would have emerged when the local folk said lang instead of long, as they do still in the lowlands of Scotland and parts of the north east of England, and as did Rabbie Burns in the well-known New Year's song, 'For Auld Lang Syne' (for old long ago). Indeed, the word lang continues to mean long in German and would have been brought to Britain in the fifth century by the conquering Angles and Saxon from their homeland on the borders of modern Germany and Denmark.

But sometime during Anglo-Saxon period and before the Norman Conquest of 1066, in the Midlands and the south of England the 'a' in lang became pronounced as an 'o', thus leading to long. Interestingly this has become the Standard English spelling and pronunciation, whereas other West Midlands dialect examples of changing an 'a' to an 'o' have not become accepted as standard.

So, in the Black Country and Birmingham – and indeed in a wider western area of England from Lancaster south to Hereford and from Derby west to Chester – the 'a' has become an 'o' in other words where the vowel precedes the letter 'n'. Consequently, in the local speech hand becomes hond and man is spoken of as mon.

According to F. W. Hackwood, that indefatigable breviter into the history of the Black Country, Langley in Anglo-Saxon times was associated with the name Walloxhall or Wallaxhale, meaning the nook or cranny of land (halh) of a chap called Wealuc. Whoever he was, Langley became part of the manor of Halas – later Halesowen – and after the Norman Conquest it was amongst the lands held by the Earl of Shrewsbury. Accordingly, along with Halesowen and Oldbury, Langley was transferred from Worcestershire to Shropshire.

A wonderful photo of folk queuing for a charabanc trip in 1919 outside 'The Snob', the picture house at Langley Institute in High Street. From the Audrey Ryan Collection.

Later, Langley was under the control of the Abbot of Halesowen Abbey and slowly a small settlement grew up in Langley Green, on the road from the abbey to Sandwell Priory. After Henry VIII dissolved the monasteries in 1534, a new manor emerged, that of Oldbury and Langley-Walloxhall, although it remained within Halesowen Parish.

For centuries, Langley and the surrounding district remained decidedly rural and was attached clearly to the biggest nearby settlement, that of Oldbury, and by the early years of the nineteenth century, the present Langley Village had not been developed. Instead there were hamlets at Langley Green, Titford Green, Rood End, Whiteheath Gate and Causeway Green.

Langley Green itself had the only place of worship locally, the Zion Independent Chapel (now the Zion United Reform Church). Founded about 1798 on a footpath leading to Causeway Green Road, the chapel arose from the meeting of like-minded Christians in the thatched cottage of James Cotterell on Langley Green Road. With a Sunday School and a growing congregation of mostly poorer working-class folk, the original chapel proved too small and so in 1828 it was replaced by a larger building – although James Cotterell remained as pastor until he died five years later.

Rood End lies between Langley Green and West Smethwick, and it is believed by many that the word rood is derived from the Holy Rood. In the Middle English period, a rood came to be associated with the wooden beams of the Cross upon which was a carved and painted figure of Christ. In medieval cathedrals and churches this Holy Rood was placed over the entrance to the choir or the chancel on a gallery, screen, or beam that spanned the chancel arch and separated it from the nave, and it was usually flanked by images of the Virgin Mary and Saint John the Evangelist.

According to local tradition, there was a Holy Rood in the open air at Rood End. It is supposed to have been placed there because the waters of a local stream contained medicinal qualities that had the power to heal the sick; and it is also said that knights on the way to the Crusades came to the brook to cleanse themselves in holy water so as to purify themselves before their quest began.

There is little hard evidence to support this legend – although that does not mean it should be dismissed out of hand. However, a more down-to-earth and plausible interpretation of the name Rood End might be that it derives from the Anglo-Saxon rod or rodu, indicating a clearing. Later a rood became an official measurement of half and acre.

As for the name End, Anglo Saxons used this term for a district of an estate, although it came to be used to denote a part of a village detached from the rest of the settlement, or else for a hamlet. Thus Rood End could be a clearing at the end of the manor. This interpretation gains strength given that Langley means the long clearing and given that Rood End is on the borders with Smethwick, which for hundreds of years was part of Harborne.

Rood End and Langley Green were noted on maps included in John Ogilby's work, *Britannia* as early as 1675, but the other hamlets locally do not seem to have appeared on maps until the early nineteenth century. By this time nailmaking had appeared in Causeway Green, where the ancient name of Penncricket Lane survives still. Hackwood asserted that this name was of Welsh origin, and certainly penn was an old Celtic word for hill – although the Anglo Saxons

Rood End Zion Anniversary Parade led by the Langley Prize Band, sometime during the inter-war years. The walkers are going along Vicarage Road from the Rood End crossroads. From the Keith Crump Collection. The Zion Chapel, Rood End was part of the Wesleyan Reform Union and dates from 1890.

Children of Arden Grove in fancy dress for the street party to celebrate the Coronation of King George VI in 1937. From the Weekly News.

also used penn for a fold or enclosure for animals. Another old route was Hobicus Lane, later to be renamed Station Road in Langley Village.

Because it was in Shropshire until the mid-1800s, Langley is rarely mentioned in old publications on the Black Country, all of which mostly focused upon the settlements in Staffordshire. Still, it is noted in F. R. Melville's *Directory of Dudley and the Mining District* of 1852. This mentions Holy Trinity Church, "a neat building situate at Langley, (which) is now in a state of completion: it is built in the Elizabethan style of architecture. The cost of erection was defrayed by a Government grant and subscription. It is capable of holding about 500 persons, and a great number of the sittings are free."

This building of Holy Trinity Church on land given by members of Park House Farm and the emergence of a new parish separate from that of Oldbury emphasised that Langley's population was growing. This expansion had been stimulated by the rapid growth of industry in the larger neighbour of Oldbury, which in itself was connected with the cutting of canals around the town – the first of which was the Birmingham Canal in 1768.

From 1835 Chance Brothers, whose world-famed glassmaking factory was in Smethwick, operated a works manufacturing soda ash and other chemicals on the canal between Oldbury and Langley Green; and from 1850, Albright and Wilson began producing phosphorus at premises nearby. Other major sources of employment in Oldbury included the tar distillation plant at Springfield, the Brade's Works, Parke's Furnace, and various mines such as Park Colliery on the edge of the South Staffordshire coalfield and close to Langley.

Melville's Directory also emphasises that despite the inward movement of people from Staffordshire, north Worcestershire and further afield, Langley Green

Pupils at Bristnall Hall Senior Boys School in Langley, who saved over £1,000 in their war savings efforts, adopted a barrage balloon – which they are inspecting in this photo taken on 24 January 1942. Pointing to the initials BHBS which had been affixed to the balloon, the officer in charge told them, "It is your balloon now".

remained the main settlement hereabouts. In 1852 Thomas Green operated there as a shopkeeper, along with three beer retailers, James Jones, John Lowe and Joseph Slimm. In fact there was little sign of the development of Langley Village, for this area boasted only Thomas Birch, who served his customers both as a beer retailer and shopkeeper. Elsewhere, David Thompson of Langley Hall acted as an agent for Burton Ales and as a storer of porter.

In addition, Langley Green boasted John Downing, a miller and farmer, and two brick works, those of Harper and Moore's – where tiles were also made - and William Titley. But brickworks were the harbingers of urbanisation, for they tended to be placed on the edges of built-up areas and so soon as they had provided the bricks for new houses and factories they disappeared under the outward march of villages that were rapidly becoming towns.

On the map included with *Jones's Mercantile Directory of the Iron District* in 1865, neither Langley nor Langley Green are noted, although Rood End Station is shown on the Stourbridge Line. This linked the Great Western Railway and the main Birmingham to Wolverhampton line on the London and North Western Railway at Galton Junction, Smethwick. Interestingly, the station itself did not actually open for another two years. However, the other nearby station was named Oldbury and Langley Green. Elsewhere in the *Mercantile Directory*, there is only one entry for Langley, the Albert Forge of John and William Bagnall, manufacturers of hammered iron.

In 1873 one of the best-known businesses in Langley was started on waste ground in Langley Green. This was Showell's Brewery at Crosswells. It is interesting that accounts of the water drawn from a well here connect with stories about Rood End and its stream of pure water. According to the Brewery owners, the spot "was well known and often visited in ancient times, on account of the wonderful and miraculous cures said to be effected by the free use of the water gushing up from the depths of the springs to be found there, and which the monks of old christened 'The wells of the Cross'." Whether or not such a legend had any base in fact, it was a good and effective marketing ploy and in a short time Showell's spectacularly increased sales of its beers, so that by 1881 it was selling to 80,000 gallons a week to licensed premises in Birmingham.

By this date, Langley Village had began to take over from Langley Green as the main shopping centre locally, and close to the new parish church there arose the High Street that became the centre of Langley and which remains so. Langley was separated from Langley Green both by the railway line and the Titford Canal. This was opened in the 1830s and linked the mines of Rowley with the Wolverhampton Level of the Birmingham Canal. Six locks at Tat Bank Road raised the level of the canal to 511 feet. Officially called the Oldbury Locks, they are known locally as the Crow or Jim Crow Locks. Just as colourful a name is that of Uncle Ben's Bridge, over the canal between Langley and Langley Green.

From the mid-nineteenth century, the number of coal miners in and about Langley increased dramatically with the opening of collieries such as the Whimsey, Valentia, Park Hall and Cinder Meadow, lying between Park Lane and Birchfield Road, and Ashes, Blackbat, Hartland and Titford between Causeway Green and Whiteheath Gate. Most of these were small, as were the other mines in the neighbourhood, and by 1896 all bar Park Hall had closed down.

The closing of the mines was matched by a growth in manufacturing, such as the Municipal Engineering Works of Ham, Baker and Company at the end of Clay Lane. As the name suggests, the business specialised in products such as valves, man-hole covers, drains for penstocks (big sluice gates) for local authorities. It was later bought out by Biwater Industries Limited.

Other prominent firms included the Langley Forge of Mill lane, founded in 1904, and which focused upon large forgings such as turbine rotors for power

This photo hangs in Langley Library and shows local children aboard a lorry at the time of celebrations of the Coronation of Queen Elizabeth II in 1953. Judith Tranter is wearing the sailor suit, and to the left is her cousin, Josephine Perry, dressed as a Quaker. Judith later joined the party held in a barn in Patrick's Field belonging to Mrs Rollinson of Causeway Green.

stations; the nearby Hughes-Johnson Stampings; MCL and Repetition Limited, small components makers; John Elwell Limited, which moved to Rood End from Birmingham between 1926 and 1930 and which made sectional steel buildings.

These metal-working companies were matched by a variety of other concerns, ranging from M. Myers and Sons, pen and office suppliers in Hall Street to the Albion Bottle Company in Rood End Road, where the bottles for HP Sauce were produced; and from the building firm of William Jackson (Langley Green) Ltd to Midland Cattle Products, which took in animal carcasses and sent out fertilisers, dripping, tallow, grease and dog food.

Despite the apparent triumph of industry in Langley, farming had not been banished. Leahouse Farm in Pound Round remained until the early twentieth century, whilst Bristnall Hall Farm and Moat Farm did not disappear beneath housing until the 1930s. Such developments came under the auspices of the Oldbury Municipal Borough, which had replaced the Oldbury Urban District in 1934. Thirty years later, Langley as part of Oldbury joined the new borough of Warley, and over the next few years redevelopment swept away many old buildings – and more were to go with the decline of manufacturing from the late 1970s. For all that, Langley retains its identity through its churches and chapels, library, parks, baths, band, pubs, High Street and above all – its people.

The photos in this chapter are taken from a cracking new book called *Playing and Performing in Langley*. Edited by Terry Daniels it has been brought out by the Langley Local History Society and published by Oldbury Local History Group. It is an absorbing work that covers a wide range of topics – from street games to spending time with the family, from playing, singing and dancing to the cinema and theatre, and from clubs, pubs and sports to pleasure grounds and public celebrations.

The book includes vivid recollections from local residents and invaluable material from the old *Weekly News*. This had begun in 1874 as the *Oldbury Weekly News*, but soon it reached out in editions for Smethwick, West Bromwich and Rowley Regis. In 1966, the Weekly News merged with the Smethwick Telephone and became the Warley News Telephone – its name reflecting the new borough of Warley into which Smethwick, Oldbury and Rowley Regis had been merged. This was closed down in 1982, although the paper was revived briefly soon after.

Playing and Performing in Langley is priced £10.00 and is available from local Sandwell libraries, 'Luv N Kissiz in High Street Langley, Black Country Books, Blackheath Market or by post by ringing 0121 558 9100 (please add £3 for post & packing).

The book is the result of the assiduous and wide-ranging research of an active and enthusiastic group, Langley Local History Society. Its two earliest publications looked at Langley, Langley Green and the surrounding areas. They were edited by Suzie Drew and Diane Callow and published by Sandwell Community Libraries.

This latest book, *Playing and Performing in Langley*, is the second of a proposed several publications that are aimed at documenting various aspects of life in and around. The first of the series was called *Making and Moving in Langley* and came out in 1999.

Terry Daniels and the Langley Local History are to be commended for their diligent investigations into the past and for their ability to reach out to a wide audience through thought-provoking and fascinating books. The Society itself meets each month and further information can be obtained from Langley Library in Barrs Street, telephone number 0121 552 1680.

Chapter 13

MAKING THE MODERN WORLD: SMETHWICK

A few years back I was a staunch supporter of the Birmingham bid to have the Millennium Dome sited in the West Midlands. Because of the problems associated with this project, both before and since its building, many people now feel that we were fortunate not to have succeeded. However, I believe that if our tender had won then we would have made it work, given that it was backed by councils in the Black Country and Solihull as well as by Birmingham and given that it was imaginative, cost-effective and based upon a superb, central location with excellent transport links.

Be that as it may, there was powerful opposition to our proposals, especially from the establishment and media in London - as there always seems to be when a good idea for a national venture is put forward by the West Midlands. On one occasion, I was invited on to the BBC Radio 4 Today programme to debate the issue with Nicholas Coleridge, a publisher and writer who was a vocal proponent of the campaign for the Dome to be placed in Greenwich, South London.

I sat in a windowless studio at Pebble Mill, connected to the London studios by earphones. As we all know, words are only part of our overall communication, for we also use our bodies, hands and eyes to 'speak', and when you cannot see your protagonist in a debate it is difficult to know when to step in and say something.

The interviewer began, as I had come to expect, with the backer of London, Mr Coleridge. He was appalled at the very suggestion that the Millennium Dome should be constructed anywhere else than in the capital and went on state that a precedent had been set by the Great Exhibition in 1851 - for would I not agree that this had been located in London. That was when my opportunity came. Mr Coleridge paused for breath – and not one to lose the chance I jumped in.

I concurred that the Great Exhibition had been held in Hyde Park in London, and added that because it was aimed to show off to the world Britain's manufacturing prowess, industrial ingenuity and economic power it had been focused on a building the like of which the world had never seen before - the Crystal Palace. A magnificent structure which struck awe into all who beheld it and which was regarded as one of the great wonders of the age, its outstanding feature was that it encompassed square feet of glass - made by the men and women of Chance's in Smethwick! And as people went into the Great Exhibition their main meeting point was a wondrous glass fountain down – crafted by the men and women of Osler's in Broad Street, Birmingham.

I could have gone on. For if the Great Exhibition proclaimed to the world that Great Britain was in a premier league of its own, unrivalled and unassailable, then the it also shouted out that Smethwick was one of the British towns that was vital to the making of the modern industrialised and urbanised world.

The Crystal Palace was an amazing structure. It was 1,851 feet long, the equivalent of 118 large eight-roomed houses, and at 456 feet was as broad as 28 such houses. The transept, the arched part that crossed the building, was 68 feet high, whilst the nave – the long part – was just three feet less in height. In all, the Crystal Palace covered almost eighteen acres, about six times that of Saint Paul's Cathedral.

Not only was it an immense size, it was groundbreaking in its style and materials. Normally, buildings were made of wood, stone or brick – the Crystal Palace owed its existence to glass and iron. It had been preceded by a handful of railway stations and large conservatories, but none compared to the Crystal Palace in their scale. Above all and crucially, the crystal that gave it the name was the result of West Midlands innovation, for Chance's of Spon Lane had to develop a new technique to develop larger panes than had been possible previously.

At 896,000 square feet, the total surface of the glass made at Chance's was a little less than I had stated on the radio – but was still astonishing – and it weighed 400 tons. Each pane of glass was large and thick – almost four and a half feet long and ten inches broad – and was joined to thin strips of wood called sash bars. This was sheet glass, which had been introduced into England by Robert Lucas Chance and James Hartley in 1832, although the difficulties associated with its production were not overcome for another six years.

In 1868 Henry Chance wrote that in the early days, because the art was new in England "foreign workmen exclusively were employed in the operation of blowing the glass, but Englishmen have been gradually initiated into the process".

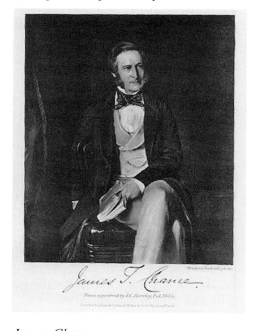

James Chance.

Chance Brothers first lighthouse optic centrally displayed at the Great Exhibition, Crystal Palace in 1851.

In particular, a French manufacturer called George Bontemps was brought to Smethwick by Robert Lucas Chance because of is expertise.

Glass making itself had been introduced to Smethwick in 1815 when Thomas Shutt had begun making crown glass at a new works he had built on part of Blakeley Hall Farm on the Birmingham Canal and west of Spon Lane. Seven years later Robert Lucas Chance bought the business. He was in partnership with a John Hartley for several years thereafter but from 1836 the firm was solely in the hands of the Chance family. Interestingly they were descended from yeomen farmers from Shepley and Burcote in the parish of Bromsgrove.

George Bontemps came to Smethwick at a crucial early stage of the development of the Chance's business. It was he who taught the English workers how to make excellent sheet glass, and later he introduced the manufacture of optical glass. It was because of this latter trade that Chance's moved into the making of lighthouse lenses, for which the company became famed.

By the year of the Great Exhibition, Chance's employed about 1,200 workers and was reputed to be the largest crown and sheet glass works in the country. It produced many of the raw materials needed for glass making, such as alkali from its own works and sand from its own pit in Leighton Buzzard. In 1868, the Smethwick works was visited by Elihu Burritt, the American consul to the West Midlands who wrote a compelling book on our region. He declared that "any American, or other foreign-born visitor will find the establishment of Messrs Chance one of the great lions of English manufacturing enterprise". He was right.

Chance's was essential to the building of the Crystal Palace and the success of the Great Exhibition. It was only surpassed in importance to the whole exciting and daring project by another Smethwick firm, Fox, Henderson and Company of the London Works, Smethwick, one of the most celebrated firms of civil engineers in the land, Described as having "the dress of a decent mechanic, the air of an educated and well-bred man, and no gloves", Charles Fox had been one of the assistants to Robert Stephenson on the construction of the London and Birmingham Railway, working first on the Watford section and then on the extension from Camden Town to Euston. On that project he had developed a new method for building skew arches and he became one of the leading experts in the use of cast iron.

In 1839 he had joined Francis Bramah in establishing a firm of engineering contractors, which had its main works at Smethwick. Two years later John Henderson became a partner in the firm that was to become Fox, Henderson & Co. It specialised in railway equipment, bridges, and structural ironwork of all kinds, and it supplied the roofs for railway stations at Paddington, Liverpool Tithebarn Street and Birmingham New Street, as well as roofs for market halls,

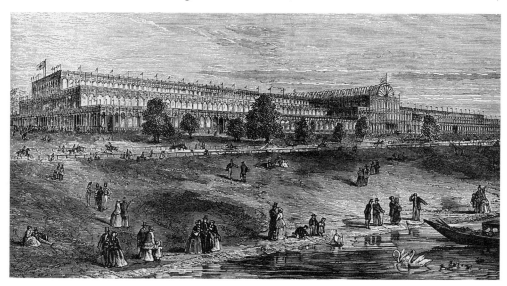

The Crystal Palace in 1851.

The Glass and Lighthouse Works at Smethwick in the early 20th century, showing glass cones across the site, from Chance Brothers & Co., Limited, 100 Years of British Glass Making 1824-1924 (Smethwick and Glasgow, Chance Brothers & Co., 1924).

slipyards and naval dockyards. The company also exported structures, amongst which were a cast-iron lighthouse to India and the iron chains for the Kiev suspension bridge.

Acclaimed for the sheer breadth of its work, Fox and Henderson also gained praise for advances in structural design. Fox himself was the designer whilst Henderson focused on the manufacturing side. For both of them, the Great Exhibition was the pinnacle of their achievements. As Fox said it had been his role to "mature and realise" Paxton's idea, but without the risk-taking of Fox and Henderson there would never have been a Crystal Palace.

In its nearly stages the two men suggested a significant change to Paxton's design, whereby an arched transept would cover the large elm trees which proved to be the great feature of the building. Fox himself then pushed forward the use of cast iron. His son recalled that "my father had great confidence in cast iron if properly designed, and he became known as the 'Cast-iron Man'. No one but he was able to design the building as regards its details, and therefore upon him, personally, devolved the duty of drawing nearly everything, even to the most minute particulars. Eighteen hours a day was he at work at the drawing-board, and, so soon as a plan was pencilled in, he sent it to the drawing-office to be traced and put in hand in the pattern shop".

Henderson meanwhile was a Scotsman who was praised as "a wonderful man of business who had the faculty of dissecting his thoughts so completely that he could dictate four different letters to four separate clerks at the same time, and know where he had left off with each letter, even to the capital letter or point of punctuation. A useful accomplishment, certainly when the art of shorthand was not practised as it now is in commercial houses."

Once the drawings left Fox they were passed on to Henderson, who directed the preparation of the iron work and other materials in Smethwick. For safety purposes, calculations were made as to the strength of the cast-iron girders and wrought-iron trusses that would hold up the building and then experiments were carried out to ensure that they were correct. Many pundits publicly expressed doubts about the stability of the Crystal Palace, but all were to be confounded by the expertise of Fox, Henderson and their workers.

Eventually, 3,300 columns were made; the same number of cast-iron girders; and 358 wrought-iron long trusses. Fox himself was at the site each day during the entire building process, from the end of July 1850 until the Great Exhibition was ready to receive goods for showing from the end of January 1851. He assigned each part to its proper position as it arrived and so ensured that the construction was finished in time. According to a contemporary, the Crystal Palace appeared to rise:

With strange suddenness. As the dry bones that were shaken by the wind came together "bone to his bone", so came the columns of this Crystal Palace! They came from afar: an exceeding great army of iron and wooden bones. By wagon loads they came, - girders and trusses, columns and ribs, of iron and wood. Then, they fitted to one another, forming a framework fairy-like and fine for the transparent glass. No unsightly heaps of brick! No smoking heaps of lime! No click of noisy trowel! No great unnecessary scaffolding! All the parts were ready prepared; and though they came from distant places, they quickly joined together like brethren who knew each other. Then, ranging in square companies, and in long rows, they helped and supported one another until they were tall and strong. Thus were they able to bear up their curved –shaped friends, the giant ribs, who gratefully formed a roof over their heads, and covered them in from the rain.

It was a staggering achievement and Fox and Henderson carried it out even though they were engaged in extensive works across the length and breadth of Britain and Ireland. They were making a railway in Ireland; a massive wrought-iron bridge across the Shannon and another over the Medway at Rochester; four large railway stations; and various other large works. Later in his description, the observer indicated the location of the "distant places" when he stated "that it was some time before the different parts came, for they had to all be cast at places near Birmingham, which are a long way off". These places were Smethwick and the Black Country.

From the end of September, wagon-load after wagon-load of columns, girders and trusses came from "the immense and mighty furnaces of the casting works" of the West Midlands, at the rate 200 columns a week. As each casting was delivered so it was weighed and examined carefully. Next it was made to bear very heavy weights, to ascertain if it was of the proper strength, after which it was painted and carried off to be fixed in its place. It amazed watchers that this procedure was carried out with such dexterity and speed that it took less than four minutes.

Fox was knighted for his invaluable contribution to the Great Exhibition and later, he and Henderson were the contractors for the removal of the Crystal Palace from Hyde Park to Sydenham in South London. Unfortunately, their business became too stretched and failed in 1856 when one of its foreign creditors could not pay it debts. Up to 2,000 people lost their jobs. It was a catastrophe for Smethwick, but the growing town showed its resilience by soon recovering from this economic disaster.

Though a small town that was still developing, the Great Exhibition emphasised to all and sundry that Smethwick was punching well above its weight on the world stage. It continued to do so because of the skills of its people and the renown of their manufactured wares.

On Wednesday 15 September 2004 I was honoured to open Smethwick's first Heritage Centre. Situated in the heart of Smethwick on the High Street next to the Council House, the opening of the centre was a dream

Kenneth Holland painted this wonderful depiction of Chance's glass works from memory. He worked there about 1940, as a lad of sixteen, "and you will find me down that hole, The Department was called the Globe and indeed that's mostly what was made. I remember the colours and the light. I have a friend who worked there as a gather, that's the chap top right with the foreman looking on, My wage was 16 shillings a week with three shifts - morning, afternoon, night. By 1941 the manufacture of cathode ray tubes for Radar and other glass ware such as test tubes and beakers, went into war production."

come true for the twenty-eight volunteers of the Smethwick Heritage Centre Trust. Members of the Trust have been working hard for over seven years to provide the people of Smethwick with a wonderful Heritage Centre which celebrates the town's proud industrial and social past.

Over those seven years many hundreds of different objects, books, photographs and memorabilia have been donated to the Trust by its generous supporters, many of which are on show in the Heritage Centre today. Artefacts on display include the many different bottles of beer produced by the mighty Mitchell's and Butler's, the cake and biscuit tins of Scribbans, a multitude of glassware manufactured at Chance Brothers glassworks, and a whole host of other items relating the industrial strength of Smethwick when firms such as Tangyes, Evereds, Guest, Keen and Nettlefold and the Birmingham Railway Carriage and Wagon Company reigned supreme in the manufacturing world.

Also on show are items that tell us about the social life of the town, for example items which relate to its schools such as the Holly Lodge Grammar Schools and the James Watt Technical School, and also to its proud sporting past when Smethwick Cricket Club was a force to be reckoned with. This unique and varied collection provides visitors with many opportunities to remember and reminisce about the past. If you want to learn more come the Centre welcomes you. Its opening times are April 1st to October 31st, Wednesday to Saturday 10am to 4pm and November 1st to March 31st, Thursday to Saturday 10am to 3pm.

Chapter 14

SHEEP FODES AND ALLEYS:
THE FOLDS OF WOLVERHAMPTON

Streets and their history are fascinating. It is impossible to delve into the past of a village, town or city without coming into contact with its street names. Usually they are confined to the older areas and they tend to be narrower, shorter and older than roads. Like an aged, wizened and shrunken person, they are filled with tales, quirks, strange happenings and puzzles. To walk down a street is to mooch with the past, to hark at the cries that once echoed there, to smell the odours that once hung hereabouts, to feel the surfaces that once textured the spot, to see the sights that once drew life to the locality and to cant with those that once dwelt nearby.

The city's landscape is shaped by its streets, roads, lanes, alleys and entries as much as it is by its natural physical features such as hills, valleys, streams and rivers; whilst the lives of its people are deeply affected by where they live, work, play and gather socially. Any business, person, family, group or event that engages the attention of those looking at the past is inevitably attached to a street or streets. So much of our history is encapsulated in the names of our streets that it is surprising that so little has been written about them as living things themselves.

Streets, roads and lanes are absorbing yet neglected. They call out to us about long dead landowners, notable figures from the history of that district and from England, local folk long forgotten, farms that have been swept away by the outpouring of the urban West Midlands, remarkable physical features, distant battles, intriguing foreign places and mysterious happenings. Such names almost demand of us that we ask questions of them.

The word street itself derives from the Latin 'strata via', meaning paved way, becoming 'straet' in Old English. The Anglo-Saxons used the term street in the names of settlements close to a Roman road, as with Streetly in Walsall and Stirchley (originally Strutley) in Birmingham. Both of these are close to the Icknield Street or Rycknield Street, which ran to the east of what was to become the Black Country – whilst the major Roman road, Watling Street, cut across to the north.

Over time, street began to be used for cuttings within settlements. Usually they were associated with main thoroughfares and often indicated the way to somewhere else. For example, most Black Country towns have a Stafford Street –

as in Dudley, Walsall, Wolverhampton, Wednesbury, Willenhall and Bilston; and a number have a Birmingham Street. Amongst them are Halesowen, Oldbury, Stourbridge and Darlaston.

Other street names common in the older parts of Black Country towns include Lichfield Street, Walsall Street, Dudley Street and Wolverhampton Street. All of these places were large settlements from the Middle Ages. There are also a few streets named after Bilston, Halesowen, Oldbury, Willenhall, Great Bridge, Tipton and West Bromwich, which were smaller in the Medieval period and which came to prominence in the nineteenth century - after the word street had begun to drop out of use and had been replaced by the expression road.

Generally, the Old English word for road was 'weg', meaning way, as in Holloway Bank, leading down from Hill Top to Bridge Street, Wednesbury and the Holyhead Road; and as in the Holloway End district of Stourbridge. By contrast the term path was used for unmade roads that went across open country.

In modern times, the word lane also raises up visions of rural settings, but in earlier periods it was often used for a narrow street in a town. Such was the case with Gads Lane, Dudley, which still comes off Wolverhampton Street; Dog Kennel Lane, Walsall which runs parallel with Lower Rushall Street; and Leve Lane, Willenhall, coming off Walsall Street.

With the expansion of the Black Country towns, urban lanes were joined by lanes that had been in the country. These were longer and often wider. There are a number of examples, including Peartree Lane on the borders of Cradley Heath and Old Hill, the nearby Waterfall Lane, and Blackbird Lane, Rowley – the expressive names of which indicate the nature of the particular route.

As for the term road, it is from the Old English word 'rad', from 'ridan', meaning to ride. This origin may explain the use of the term 'oss road' by Black Country folk when warning their children "to mind the 'oss road" or advising someone to "keep out the oss road". Road occurs only once in Shakespeare's works and it remained unusual until the eighteenth century, except in connection with national highways.

One such was the road from London to Shrewsbury, which ran through Birmingham and Smethwick and went on through Oldbury, Tividale, Dudley and Himley. By the early 1700s it was disused and had been replaced by one that went from Birmingham, probably through West Bromwich and then via Wednesbury and Bilston and Wolverhampton. After 1815, this became part of the 'Parliamentary' mail coach road. This linked the port of Holyhead in Anglesey, and hence Dublin and Ireland, with London and it led to the appearance of a Holyhead Road between Moxley and Wednesbury and to another between West Bromwich and Handsworth.

The road was supervised by the great engineer Thomas Telford who improved it markedly by using Rowley Rag stone for the surface instead of clinkers and slag, the waste from furnaces. He also constructed short by-passes at Wednesbury and Bilston and made a better way at Tettenhall. This had been crooked, narrow and steep but Telford redesigned the road through cuttings and embankments.

In the second half of the 1700s, the use of road grew after with the building of military routes in Scotland and turnpikes in England. Administered by trusts authorised by private acts of Parliament to levy tolls on travellers, turnpikes took their name from a pike that formed a barrier to traffic and that was turned to allow access.

One of the earliest turnpike acts in the Black Country was passed in 1748 for "repairing road from Sutton Coldfield Common to Walsall". Its main concern was not for long distance travellers but for the needs of local traders. Three turnpikes came out from Walsall to bring it into easier contact with surrounding areas so that "the price of the carriage of goods might be reduced". Eleven years later another act allowed the repairing and widening of roads to and from Bilston.

North Street, probably in the 1930s, looking down from Saint Peter's Walk on the left. On the right and in the middle, the two large buildings are the 'Old Mitre Hotel and Jessup's Hotel, between which lay the entrance for Mitre Fold. All the photos for this article are taken from Anthony Perry, The Folds of Wolverhampton (Brewin Books: 2005) and are by courtesy of Wolverhampton Archives and Local Studies. Priced £12.95 The Folds of Wolverhampton is available from bookshops and Saint Peter's Collegiate Church bookshop, between 10am and 4pm.

For many years the word road was restricted to these main roads that led to other places. In Walsall, the Birmingham Road was the extension of Birmingham Street; the Wednesbury Road carried on from Bradford Street; Wolverhampton Street became the Wolverhampton Road; Lichfield Road was the continuation of Lichfield Street; and Stafford Street ran into the Bloxwich Road.

As this and other towns grew, so too did the better off citizens follow these roads. They wanted to move away from the cramped, smoky, polluted and overcrowded centres and into drier, healthier spot that afforded good views. Often these were on higher ground and were upwind of factories. With the flight of the more prosperous, the gardens and open spaces in the town centres were filled in with workshops and back-to-back and other poor quality houses. This infilling increased the fumes and crimping and led to the negative connotation of streets as older parts where the poor lived in decrepit housing amidst pollution. Regarded as short, narrow and unpleasant, the word street became unattractive and was shunned by house builders from the later nineteenth century. The use of lane also suffered from the prejudice of the prosperous, as did alleys, entries and passageways.

These, too, are intriguing, leading as they do almost mysteriously from one place to another but yet having a life of their own. Too small to impact on a wider area, such little throughways draw us into a highly localised world, dragging us away from the global to the day-to-day life of a specific and small place. Too often in our redevelopments, streets, alleys, entries and passageways have been erased from history - and with them has gone not only the look of the past but also its feel. Fortunately, Wolverhampton retains a number of these captivating places, many of which have a distinctive local name – fold.

Throughout the Black Country, fode is used for a yard. Derived from the term sheep fold it continued to have a vigour in the urban and industrial setting generations after its original meaning had been swept away. However, in Wolverhampton fold refers not to a yard but to the alleys, passages and little streets found in the oldest parts of the city.

Not that folds are absent elsewhere. The Fold is to be found in both Darlaston and Penn, and also in Kings Norton, Birmingham; whilst there is a Wakelams Fold off Louise Street in Gornal. But nowhere else has so many folds as Wolverhampton. Today, they call us back to the beginnings of the city and thanks to the perseverance, dedication and skilful research of Anthony Perry, their significance has been brought to the fore.

There would seem little doubt that the word arose from the wool trade, and of course, Wolverhampton was a major centre of that trade. In the sixteenth century, it had many clothiers and drapers who oversaw a variety of workers who actually produced the cloth: from the picking of wool through combing, washing, spinning, weaving, fulling, dying to finishing. In addition, Wolverhampton boasted a number of Merchants of the Staple. These belonged to the Society of Staplers, the oldest corporation of merchants in England, and were allowed to buy and sell the raw wool.

As late as the end of the eighteenth century and despite industrialisation and the decline of the wool trade locally, Wolverhampton still had people making their livings from wool and cloth.

For all that the Medieval town was so important in the wool trade, it is not known if the original purpose of the city's folds was for the gathering of sheep. Still, all of them were immediately off the main routes into Wolverhampton in the Middle Ages and are close to places of importance for the trade. Townwell Fold emphasises this. In the eighteenth century it ended at a small enclosed field, Cock Close, where cloth was hung on hooked supports called tenterhooks. Next to The Tenters was the Puddle Brook and linen well, both of which provided water for cleaning wool and cloth. It would not be surprising for a sheep fold to be hereabouts.

Diligently, enthusiastically and sympathetically, Anthony Perry has delved into the history of Wolverhampton through the folds of the city. In doing so he brings from

Women of Skinner Street in the later nineteenth century. This street emerged in 1861, before then it was the middle section of Townwell Fold. Today this site is Victoria Fold.

the mists of the past into the glare of history people long dead, events long forgotten and trades long gone. His new book *The Folds of Wolverhampton* is a remarkable work for it is written by a man who is infused with a love of his city and with a passion for bringing its story into the present and future. It reaches back successfully into the Middle Ages and bonds the city of the twenty-first century with its roots. Most of all, The Folds of Wolverhampton is a tribute to those who lived, worked, played, laughed and cried in the heart of one of England's great urban centres.

Anthony and his wife, Joyce, are distinguished historians of Wolverhampton – distinguished because they have devoted themselves to making Wulfrunians alert to aspects of their history that were in danger of disappearing from view. They have written widely and successfully on topics such as the Collegiate Church of Saint Peter's and the novelist, Ellen Fowler, and this book on the folds of Wolverhampton represents another achievement.

Anthony's urge to write was impelled by his great grandfather, Francis Weetman, who was a self-taught scholar and lover of books, and by his own upbringing in the middle of Wolverhampton. In the 1950s, his family lived in Red

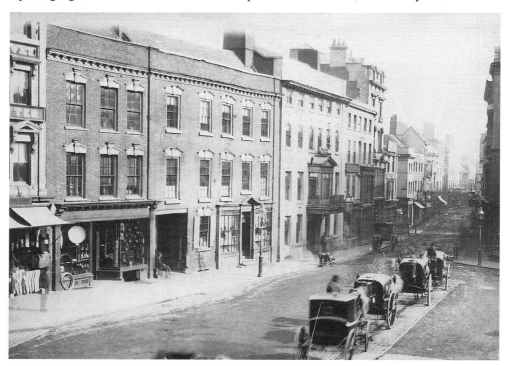

High Street, otherwise Queens Square, in the 1860s. The arched entrance on the left leads to Swan Yard and Wheelers Fold.

Looking along Market Street from Queen Street in the 1920s. Behind the policeman and to his right is Rawlins the hairdresser. Beyond that is the Wolverhampton Brewery Company and the start of Castle Yard.

Lion Street and as he explains, "the lower end of Paternoster Row opened out on to the street, but not for vehicles. The families in the street did not refer to it as Paternoster Row – it was just 'the alley'.

"There was a low brick wall with railings set into it and an opening in the middle, about the right width to have had a gate hung, and a step down on to the pavement. The opening always seemed to be large enough for the ball to bounce out on to the street, just at the right time for a car to have to brake, and then we children would have to mutter 'sorry' to an annoyed driver."

From an early age short, narrow access-ways made an impact upon Anthony and in this book he takes us with him as he traipses around them, starting and finishing in Wulfruna Street, between the Civic Centre and the main University buildings.

The first stop is Wadham's Fold, the newest of all folds as it was created in 1978 when the Civic Centre was completed. Running down a slope from the Saint Peter's Square end of Wulfuna Street to North Street, this is "no more than a footway" but it recalls "a street lost as a result of the construction of the Ring Road in the 1960s and 1970s. Wadham's Hill descended about 35 feet (11 metres) in height from its junction with North Street, where there was a large area used for parking in front of the Molineux Hotel, and where a row of houses was actually called Molineux Fold, down to a traffic light controlled crossroads with Waterloo Road and a tree-lined Bath Road."

The line of the street was in existence in 1750, as indicated on Isaac Taylor's Map, although it was the bank itself that was called Wadham's Hill. Whoever Wadham was is lost, but in 1817 William Pitt mentioned that there was an ancient arched well at Waddam's-hill, called Meg-a-doodle's-well, but by then it was neglected.

Not far away is Mitre Fold, going between Red Lion Street and North Street, which had been called Goat or Tup Street. According to Anthony "this may be our first link with the wool trade. The word tup, meaning a male sheep or ram, was in use from the 13th Century, and perhaps a sheep market was sited here." Now

The back fold called Giffard Arms Yard, running from Victoria Street to Townwell Fold, in the 1920s. Notice the line of washing and the communal facilities, like the lavatories and brewus, on the left.

widened, Mitre Fold once was just three yards wide and was approached by steps from Red Lion Street. At its North Street end it had Jessop's licensed hotel on one corner and the Old Mitre temperance hotel on the other. Previously a pub, the Old Mitre's plot included fifteen small cottages that ran the length of the fold and which had a shared, shallow yard at the back that was approached from one, central entry.

In 1750, Mitre Fold was shown as Mill Alley. By 1827 it had become Mitre Fold and its cottages were present. Anthony proposes that because the lower end of the fold was narrow and dropped to Red Lion Street (originally Green Hill Walk), "it would be very difficult to use it for animals, but if Tup Street was so named for the reason that it was used for a sheep market in early days, then the upper part of the Fold, before the cottages were built, could have been convenient for the temporary penning of animals pending their showing and sale".

North Street itself was the site of Wolverhampton's Town Hall until 1978 when the Civic Centre was finished. Now the Magistrates' Court, this was the main Council offices from the 1870s. Before then, the Red Lion Inn stood here, hence Red Lion Street. Adjoining it was a property that was owned by Henry, Duke of Cleveland, thus Cleveland Street, who was married to Lady Sophia Powlett, recalled in Powlett Street.

Cleveland was the Lord of the Manor of the Prebend of Wobaston. A prebend was an estate that belonged to a cathedral or collegiate church, such as Saint Peter's, and a prebendary was a churchman attached to that place of worship who benefited from that estate. Cleveland's property abutted Blossom's Fold, which had been the location of the house of the Prebend of Wobaston. In the fourteenth century two of the prebendaries, clergymen, had been called de Blastom or de Blaston, which led to Blassoms Foulde in 1609 and Blossoms Court by 1750.

Anthony Perry's book unfolds the people of Wolverhampton as much as it unfolds the folds of the city. Each page opens up something captivating. There is the connection of the first store of James Beattie in Victoria Street with the ancient Townwell Fold; the link of Jabez Tunnicliff, the founder of the Band of Hope, with Summer Row; the bond between Waterstone's in Farmer's Fold with the drapery emporium of Bedford Williams; and the tie between Woolpack Alley and the Levesons, staplers in the town in the early 1500s. *The Folds of Wolverhampton* is a book that all of us will learn from and enjoy, but above all it is a book of which Wulfrunians should be proud.

Chapter 15

NAILS AND COAL: BURNTWOOD

Burntwood in Staffordshire and Brandwood End on the south west of Birmingham: at first sight there appears to be no connection between them. They are two communities separated not only geographically by the urban sprawl of the West Midlands but also by distinct histories and developments. Burntwood is a former mining area embedded in an agricultural setting, whilst Brandwood was a rural location until the inter-war years when its fields were cut through by roads and overlain with houses.

Yet for all the diversity between them, Burntwood and Brandwood share something that ties them together irrevocably: the origins of their place names. Brandwood End, the southernmost area of Kings Heath, takes its last name from the Anglo-Saxon term used for a district of an estate or part of a village that was detached from the main settlement – in this case Kings Norton; whilst Brandwood is derived from the Middle English word 'brende', meaning burnt, and the Anglo-Saxon term 'wodu', a wood. It may be that wood was burned here for charcoal or that the word itself was burned - whatever the case a document from 1519 noted that a William Roper was living at Brande Ende.

As for Burntwood, in 1296 it was recorded that the bishop of Coventry and Lichfield had 300 acres of common pasture in Brendewode. This name indicates that Burntwood, too, traces its beginnings back to the words brende and wodu. In his book on Staffordshire Place Names in 1902, W. H. Duignan puts forward an interesting explanation for how Brendewode arose. He cited a Forest Jury of 1262 which found that "a certain heath was burnt by the vill of Hammerwich to the injury of the king's game".

The forest and game related to Cannock Chase or Cannock wood, as it was often called, the great medieval royal hunting ground that is thought to have stretched from Sutton Coldfield almost to the entrance of Lichfield. Three miles to the south west of the cathedral city of which it was a village, Hammerwich itself is an intriguing name. It is probable that it signifies the hammer work or trading place, from the Anglo-Saxon words hamor and wic, and suggests some form of manufacturing locally. In the Middle Ages, and afterwards, land was often cleared for cultivation by burning and it seems that this may have been what the people of Hammerwich did to nearby heathland and woodland, an action forever recalled in Burntwood.

By the later seventeenth century the name had changed slightly to Burndwood, from which Burntwood emerged. The shift in name is related to metathesis, that linguistic process that saw Birmingham also become known as Brummagem. Metathesis means that two sounds that appear in a particular order in one form of a word occur in the reverse order in a related form of the word. In the case of Birmingham the 'r' and 'i' in 'Bir' were reversed, a feature that occurred often; for example the word bird was 'brid' in Anglo Saxon and thus in 1200 a property transaction noted Brimingham.

However, the vowel sound at the start of Birmingham could also be spelled as an 'e' or 'u', making Bermingham or Burmingham, each of which could become Bremingham or Brumingham. This development was made plain in 1189 when a document spelled the surname of the Bermingham family (the lords of Birmingham) as de Brummingeham.

Finally, another linguistic change also had an affect, whereby 'agem' replaced 'ingham'. This was frequent in names where 'ing' is followed by a final syllable beginning with 'h' or 'w'. Thus Brummingegham became Brymecham in 1402 and Brummagem by the 1640s.

A Sunday School Parade in 1909, going down the High Street in Chasetown . The Wesleyan Chapel is on the left. The photos in this article are taken from Ron Bradbury, Nails, Coal and the People of Old Burntwood. The book captures the spirit of Burntwood, Chasetown and Chase Terrace in 200 old photographs. It is available from Burntwood Post Office, Swan Island, Burntwood and costs £8.00, or from the author with free post and packing at 01543 450711 or Ron Bradbury, 74 Biddulph Park, Chase Terrace, Burntwood, WS7 1LQ.

With regard to Burntwood it would seem that the 'e' of Brendwode became a 'u', leading to Brundwood in 1517; and that the 'u' later swapped places with the 'r' in local speech, making Burndwood by 1680 and then Burntwood.

During the Reformation of Henry VIII, when the king dissolved the monasteries and convents and appropriated to himself religious buildings and lands, much of what became Burntwood was taken from the Bishop of Coventry and Lichfield. In 1546 it was sold to Sir William Paget, whose descendants remained the major land owners until the twentieth century as first the Barons Paget and then the Earls of Uxbridge and lastly the Marquesses of Anglesey.

I have scoured in vain the early histories of Staffordshire by Robert Plot (1686) and the Reverend Stebbing Shaw (1801) for any references to Burntwood. Similarly there is nothing noted of the place in Erdeswicke's *Survey of Staffordshire* carried out between 1553 and 1663, although there is a short comment in the Reverend Thomas Harwood's edition of that work in 1844. It is surprising there is not more given that as vicar of Saint Mary's Lichfield, Harwood was patron of the chapel in Burntwood. This entry states that:

> At Burntwood was erected a chapel, 1819, under the benevolent auspices of Dean Woodhouse, for the use of a numerous population, which had been to this time precluded from any place of worship, this hamlet being at the inconvenient distance of four miles from the parish church.
>
> Fuliten, in this hamlet, is the property of Thomas Birch Reynardson, a lieutenant-general, who married, June *3*, 1806, Ethelred-Anne ... He inherited this property from the Birches his paternal ancestors. Burntwood, is firewood, from the Saxon, brennan, to burn.

A Great War hero feted in High Street. Some people believe that the soldier was called Whitehouse.

Closely associated with Burntwood was Ediall, which "was once possessed by the families of Wolferstan, Ridding, and Burnes. From them it passed to Thomas Hammond, who built the hall in which Dr. Samuel Johnson resided in 1736. It passed to Fettiplace Nott, esq. to Thomas Ashmole-, and to John Fern, whose younger son, Robert, sold it, and the house was taken down in 1809."

Johnson, "that eminent lexicographer" ran a school for a couple of years at Ediall Hall, a square brick mansion with a cupola and balustrades. Here he taught David Garrick, who became the most famous actor of his time and who is recalled in the theatre named after him in Lichfield. But according to William White's *History, Gazeteer and Directory of Staffordshire* (1834), "not meeting with sufficient encouragement Johnson did not long remain in this obscure situation". In 1737 he and Garrick moved to London, but it is believed that Johnson's Black servant continued to have a school somewhere in Burntwood.

White included a short reference about Burntwood in his full section on Lichfield. He explained that together with Edgehill (Ediall, which was also written as Edjall) and Woodhouses, it was one of "three hamlets of straggling houses, forming a joint township and chapelry, on the eastern side of Cannock Chase", extending from 1½ to 3 miles west and west by and south of Lichfield".

Wodehousleye was recorded in 1374, and suggests houses in a woodland clearing; whilst the stretch of the Lichfield road east of Burntwood was known as Edial Lane by 1409. If it is derived from Edge Hill then it would mean the hill called Edge, although edge itself was the Anglo-Saxon word for an escarpment.

White's entry added that "besides an extensive common right on the Chase, Burntwood contains 709, Edgehill 360, and Woodliouses 13389 acres of land, all in a good state of cultivation. The Marquis of Anglesey is lord of Burntwood, and has also *a* paramount jurisdiction in Edgehill and Woodhouses, of which S. P. Wolverston, Esq. of Stratford, is the mesne lord; but here are many smaller freeholders."

On the Chase itself was an extensive rabbit warren "with a neat house called Coney Lodge". Of course, coney is the old word for rabbits, and is used still by Americans. James Derry was the warren keeper. Other large houses included Maple-hayes, "the pleasant seat of John Atkinson", and Pipe Hall, "an ancient manor house, now occupied by a farmer". Both were in Woodhouses, as was Ashenbrooke "an ancient farm-house with some curious relics of stained glass in its windows."

In 1884 Maple Hayes and 455 acres of its 1,010 acre estate was sold to Albert Octavius Worthington, a partner in the Burton Upon Trent brewing firm of Worthington and Co. The Worthington Estate was built up in succeeding years to reach over 1500 acres and in 1949, when William Worthington Worthington died, most of it was sold to a trust.

Apart from its chapel, "a small brick edifice", Burntwood in the 1830s also had a free school that provided an education for the poor children of the hamlet and those of Edial, Woodhouses and Hammerwich. The school had been endowed with £600 by Elizabeth Ball. The sum of £200 had been spent in building the place, whilst the remaining £400 was "secured on a farm, in Burntwood, belonging to General Reynardson, and now occupied by Thomas Derry". The yearly interest of £40 was paid to the schoolmaster

Another benefactor to the poor was William Cadman. In 1705 he had bequeathed the rent of 20 shillings from a cottage and its garden to be used to pay for two sermons to be preached at Hammerwich Chapel on the first Sunday in Lent and the Sunday after Saint James's Day. The remainder was to be distributed amongst the local poor.

By this date, 1834, Burntwood had a population of around 750 and just a few shopkeepers. They were Edward Asbury, and Henry Webb and William Meeson – both of whom were victuallers and butchers. These were outnumbered by licensees: Francis Newell Horton kept the Three Horseshoes beer house; James Littler doubled up as a tailor and beer house keeper; Thomas Salt ran the Lord Nelson; and Josiah Sanders had the Nags Head.

There were also a number of tradesmen in Burntwood. They were Richard Atkins, a nailmaker; Thomas Littler, a tailor; Richard Snape, a wheelwright; Barnaby Craddock and Thomas Horton, shoemakers; and William Rock, a blacksmith. Their numbers were supplemented in Woodhouses by Mrs Elizabeth Asbury, a shopkeeper and George Gettey, a blacksmith; and in Edgehill by John Williams, a shopkeeper, Thomas Berrisford, a wheelwright, James Burton a shoemaker, and William Robinson, a brickmaker.

But the most prominent feature locally was the number of small and large farmers. There were 27 in total. Several of them were obviously related: three farms were run by William, Thomas and James Derry; two by William and John Ashmale; and another two by John and William Tudor. Given the importance of farming, it is apparent that most of the rest of the population must have been working as farm labourers or as skilled agricultural workers.

Within twenty years, the social and economic make-up of Burntwood and its district had been changed. Farming remained important, but mining was now becoming a major source of employment and was drawing in newcomers from the coalfields of East Shropshire, South Staffordshire and elsewhere. In 1850, the Marquis of Anglesey opened a colliery at nearby Hammerwich and extended to it a branch from the canal. Within the next few years, more coal mines were sunk on the heathland of the Chase and there appeared two new villages connected strongly to Burntwood: Chasetown and Chase Terrace.

At first called Cannock Chase, Chasetown developed on the Rugeley Road, which ran north across the heath. It lay just to the east of a mine that was opened in

Miners at work.

1852 and which was approached via Colliery Road, later named Church Street. By 1867 the village had gained its modern name and some people attribute this to George Poole, vicar of Burntwood.

By this time, the mines on the Chase had been sold by the Angleseys to the Cannock Chase Colliery Company (1858), formed by J. R. McLean and Richard Chawner. McLean was civil engineer who had been a consultant on the Suez Canal and who leased the South Staffs railway; whilst Chawner had formed the South Staffs Waterworks Company. The company sank new mines north of Chasetown, on the south side of Cannock Road, and another new mining village appeared for the miners and their families. Called Chase Terrace, it was north of Cannock Road and west of Rugeley Road, and by 1881 its people numbered nearly 2,000. Boney Hay was also associated with Burntwood and expanded in the nineteenth century. Called 'le Burnehew' in 1361 it lies west of Ogley Hay Road

In 1959, just over 100 years after the first mine hereabouts had opened, the last one was closed. Once again Burntwood was faced with dramatic social and economic change as it became an overspill area for Birmingham and the Black Country. Between 1961 and 1971 its population nearly doubled as firms relocated there to a large industrial estate. Amongst them was Benton and Stone. My Nan, Lil Perry, had worked there when the firm was in Miller Street, Aston, up past the Norton Motorbike factory.

My earliest memory of Burntwood was when Our Nan took me and Our Kid as seven and eight year olds on a bus trip in an attempt to find the new factory so as to meet some of her old pals. We traipsed around for what seemed like hours but never did find Benton and Stone!

Today part of Lichfield District Council, Burntwood with Chasetown, Chase Terrace and Boney Hay is as big as the ancient city. With the Burntwood Town Shopping Centre and market opened in 1970 and its library and parish council offices in use from 1987, modern Burntwood seems a new place. It is not and thanks to the efforts of Ron Bradbury and others its past will not be forgotten.

The photos in this feature are taken from his pioneering book, *Nails, Coal and the people of Old Burntwood* (2003). Ron is tremendous historian,

The rear of Tub and Bucket Row, on Nags Hill (Rugeley Road). Burntwood. Thanks to June E. Thomas, who was born and raised there and who spent the first couple of years of her marriage there from 1958. The first lady is June's Aunt Nellie and the second, in the light coloured dress, is Lizzie Lee. There were five houses in Tub and Bucket Row and June wonders "can you imagine some of these properties had seven or more children raise din them, never the less everyone generally had a good life, in fact in my time the whole of the row was related in some way".

The name of Tub and Bucket Row "was actually coined by the locals in passing the row when tubs and buckets were on view outside to catch the rain water cascading from the downspouts. In those days it was stored and used around the home. This was a precious commodity because it was very soft. Indeed I remember it being used on many occasions to wash my hair. Although in my days we did have cold water on tap I suppose in the early years of the row there would have been a communal pump. I remember my childhood there with great affection and the arrival of a baby sister some time after Dad came home from the Second World War. Sadly she is no longer with us but memories of Tub and Bucket Row still linger."

who is devoted to ensuring that the past of Burntwood is brought to the fore at a time when there is so much change in and around Cannock Chase. The closure of the mines locally and the decline of the old ways have been accompanied by the migration into the area of new families. Ron and a number of other determined local historians are carrying out a vital task in alerting old and new residents to the history of Burntwood. In so doing they are emphasising a sense of continuity that is so essential for the well-being of any community.

Ron Bradbury is the front of the wheelbarrow in the lead of this race at the sports day of Burntwood Infant and Junior School in 1950.

Ron makes the point that "because Burntwood Town consists of several villages, each area of the town has its own heritage and story to tell. Burntwood, Edial and Woodhouses and also adjacent Hammerwich are ancient villages and made a living by agriculture and later nail-making. The mining of coal by the Marquis of Anglesey in the mid 1800s at Norton Pool and the take over of the collieries by John Robinson McClean and Richard Croft Chawner put two new villages on the map; Chasetown and Chase Terrace, with their own histories to tell."

Ron is also an active member of two significant local groups: the Burntwood Chase Heritage Group and the Keepers of the Archive. The Heritage Group is run by a dedicated and highly-motivated group volunteers, the aim of whom is to preserve and promote the heritage of Burntwood and the surrounding villages from the time of William the Conqueror onwards. All aspects of Burntwood history are collected for future generations and the BCHG has a display within the Old Mining College Centre in Queen Street, Chasetown, which is open to view every weekday and free to visit.

The Group meets once a month from 7.00 p.m. at St. John's Church, High Street, Chase Terrace during the winter months. This meeting is followed by a Film Night for the general public. This usually starts with a comedy film or two, and after a short tea/coffee break, continues with a longer film or a slide presentation with a historical theme. The public are always welcome to join the Group and help its members with their activities. Tea and biscuits are served in the interval. Admission is £2.00 with a 50% discount to members. There is also a website, www. Burntwoodchaseheritage.co.uk

As for the Keepers of the Archive, this was formed in April 1999 as a local history group covering Burntwood, Chasetown and Chase Terrace. The Archive itself is a collection of photographs and memories of the area. Anyone in the area can loan the 'Archive' free of charge. The group also hold occasional slide shows and similar fund-raising event, but its main objective is to continue both to collect and take photographs of the area and memories of local people, and to erect plaques at local sites of interest. The Keepers have an important and informative website that is linked to the Heritage Group website.

Chapter 16

GRAVELLY PLACE
TO GREAT BRIDGE

The story goes that in 1646, in the English Civil War, Parliamentarian troops were bent upon taking the Royalist stronghold of Dudley Castle. For four years, under the command of Colonel Levison, a large landowner around Wolverhampton and Wednesfield, it had been a stronghold for the supporters of the king, but that was all to change. On their way to attack the castle, soldiers loyal to Parliament crossed the River Tame at the bridge at Great Bridge. The crossing point was only wide enough to take a horse and its rider, but it was robust enough to withstand the passage of a large number of men and beasts one after another. So impressed was the officer in charge by the bridge's sturdiness, that he proclaimed that henceforth it should be known as a "great bridge".

That small bridge, for such it is, is still there at the back of Fisher Street, and although the Parliamentarians may well have gone across it, there is no evidence to support the tale of its naming - good as it is. So then, how did the bridge become great and thus give its name to Great Bridge, that place that straddles the Tame and as such is half in West Bromwich and half in Tipton? As far back as 1550 a bridge is mentioned as the crossing of the river hereabouts, and it is likely that such a structure goes back even further. Because of its importance in linking West Bromwich and Tipton, the bridge was looked after by both places. But it had a wider significance. It was part of the route from London to Shrewsbury and was also used for the carrying of coal.

In the later seventeenth century that road followed the line of the present Whitehall Road before it bends at Sheepwash Lane, and then went straight on across the modern Slater Street and Fisher Street. Due to the passage of numerous heavy loads, it was in a poor state and so long-distance traffic moved to an alternative road via Smethwick and Dudley. Still in 1699 the route through Great Bridge was declared to be part of the 'great road' between London, Chester and Shrewsbury. Some people assert that the bridge's location on this great road gave rise to the name Great Bridge, but this is also unlikely.

In 1699 and in recognition of the bridge's importance to communications in Staffordshire as a whole, a contribution of £50 was made by the county towards converting the bridge so as to allow the passage not only of horses but also of carts

Crowds on the corner of Aston Street and Toll End Road during the wedding of Elsie Norton and Charles Arnold in 1949. Amongst the onlookers on the back row left to right are Margaret Bryant, Florence Reeves, Audrey Patrick, Alma Partridge, Iris Ward, Betty Shelley, Doris Whitehouse, Mary Barklam, Cissy Jenkins, Ken Ralphs, Nellie Whitehouse and Joan Butler. On the front row are Pauline Ince, Maureen Nicklin, Colleen Nicklin and Margaret Garner. Thanks to Elise Arnold.

Mind you the people in charge of West Bromwich were not that keen on joining in the scheme. That caused real problems and so in 1702 the court ordered the repayment of £20 of the county's grant. As a result the remaining £30 was spent on the Tipton half of the bridge and on a causeway leading to it from that place. The work was finished by 1706, but it seems that it must have cost more than anticipated, because Tipton complained that it had been put in debt and successfully claimed back its outgoings.

The improvements and a speeding up of economic activity led to a marked increase in the traffic that went across the bridge and by the 1720s it was stated that it carried much coal, iron and lime. These were three of the most important minerals mined in the Black Country and were essential to the socio-economic transformation of Britain during the Industrial Revolution. And as the impact of industrialisation began to gather pace, the bridge was taken away from Tipton and West Bromwich and responsibility for its upkeep was handed over to Staffordshire. In 1780 the county rebuilt the bridge just a short way from the small bridge. This move led to a realignment of the road as it is today, running up from Whitehall Road into Great Bridge Street and thence across the Tame to New Road. Much later this crossing point was widened, but the eighteenth-century work formed part of the northern part of the bridge well into the later twentieth century.

So if there was a bridge that was made bigger, or greater, did this give rise to the name Great? No, it did not. The answer lies in Anglo-Saxon place names. In the later Middle Ages, a large part of the south-western district West Bromwich was called Greet. There is a similar place in Birmingham and both share the same meaning. They are derived from the Anglo-Saxon word 'greot' meaning a gravelly place. Interestingly, Greet in Birmingham is an area alongside the River Cole, whilst Greet in West Bromwich was alongside the River Tame.

Charles Clee's general store, 78, New Road, about 1922. Left to right are Harry Perks, Rene Clee, Arthur Perks and Leslie Taylor. Thanks to Alf Perks. The shop was later run by Samuel Ashcroft.

In the 1290s, mention was made in a document of Greet Mill. This stood further south of the modern Great Bridge, about where West Bromwich Street crosses the Tame. However, even earlier, in the late twelfth century, there is evidence of another mill at Grete, as it was spelled. This belonged to the lord of the manor and was given by him to Sandwell Priory. It is not known exactly where this mill was, but it may have been just to the south of Great Bridge.

Whatever the location of the mill, the name Grete became linked with the bridge, as documents from the sixteenth and seventeenth centuries make plain; whilst in this locality the Tame was also called the Grete Brook. It seems that in this area, Greet could be pronounced Great for in a deed from 1556 mention was made of land 'between the King's highway leading from Greate Green to the town of Duddele'. Despite this, Greets Green continued to hold on to the old name of Greet, and was noted as such in the same century. Interestingly, a map of 1682 spells the place as Grits Green, as it is pronounced today. That map also names Great Bridge as a hamlet of Tipton, although the earliest settlement had grown up on the West Bromwich side of the Tame in the middle decades of the sixteenth century.

Be that as it may, for many years there was only a small population locally, as there was in the districts of Greets Green, Swan Village and Ryders Green, which probably recall the Rider family who owned the Dunkirk Estate and who are brought to mind in Ryder Street and Dunkirk Avenue. But as much of South Staffordshire sloughed off its rural nature and began to assert itself industrially, Great Bridge was set to become a place with an identity of its own.

The onset of manufacturing locally was associated with Edward Elwell, recalled now in Elwell Street. His father, another Edward, had operated a foundry in a former water mill at Hateley Heath, in the era before the widespread use of steam engines, and when water was vital to power large machinery. From 1809 Edward Elwell junior was operating an iron foundry at Great Bridge. It is likely that he had been encouraged to set up there by the closeness of canals, that vital form of communication for a landlocked region that did not boast a large and navigable river.

The Birmingham Canal was critical to this process of reaching out. It allowed the swift, cheap and efficient import of Black Country coal and iron to Birmingham, and had been opened fully in 1772. However, three years before that the Balls Hill Branch Line had been ready for use. This linked the Birmingham Canal at Spon Lane with Wednesbury. A local canal system was developed upon this branch, and in 1786 another branch from Ryders Green through to Great Bridge and thence to Wednesbury was opened. Finally, in 1833 the Haines Branch was opened from Great Bridge to enable access to the mines in the south west of West Bromwich.

One of these was the Cop Hall Colliery owned by Haines and Horton. In 1836 workers at a pair of pits here raised 1,000 tons of coal, a record in England. Another was Great Bridge Colliery. Like many Black Country pits it was badly affected by flooding, and it was abandoned as waterlogged in the 1840s; although in 1873 the West Bromwich Colliery Company was formed to drain and reopen the Great Bridge Colliery. By this date, tube making was also prominent in Great Bridge, as was the production of blue and red bricks, whilst one of the biggest concerns locally was that of Solly Brothers, the Great Bridge Iron and Steel Company, which also had works in Toll End. In 1898 this "important works which has a reputation far and wide" was taken on by Messrs Roberts and Cooper.

Great Bridge was also firmly placed on the railway map of England. On the South Staffordshire Line, Great Bridge North Railway Station had opened in 1850 as the first such facility in Tipton; and from 1866 the Great Bridge Branch of the Birmingham, Wolverhampton and Dudley Railway allowed connections to the rest of the West Midlands This was closed 98 years later.

The growth of employment led inexorably to a rise in population. The Greets Green and Sheepwash Lane areas were urbanized from the 1830s – although the names of both continue to call to us of their rural origins. Great Bridge itself was described as a large village in 1834 in the *History, Gazeteer and Directory of Staffordshire*. According to this publication, 'less than 40 years ago, there were only eight houses between Great-Bridge and the Bull's Head (West Bromwich) a distance of two miles, which now forms almost one continued street of buildings, with various cross-streets branching from it at irregular distances'.

Within another twenty years Cop Hall Street – as it then was - had emerged running down from Sheepwash Lane. This neighbourhood of back-to-back and other old houses was cleared from 1959 and replaced by a new council estate. Just up from the junction of Whitehall Road with the Oldbury Road, Grout Street was also obvious by the 1850s, along with Finch Street, Frances Street and Rogers Street. Together they were known as Paul's New Town and then just as New Town, after Sir Horace St Paul, a Northumberland grandee who also owned the Pump House Estate between Dunkirk and Great Bridge. Early on, one of the streets was renamed Farley Street. Another was later called Horton Street and the third has now disappeared.

Development locally gathered momentum. In 1853 the Dunkirk Estate had just a few cottages, piggeries and brewhouses. That changed swiftly when part of the property was put up for sale. It was advertised as good investment because of the demand by miners and others for houses. Some of estate was bought by a Birmingham building society and was split up into small building plots. By 1854 the society was seeking buyers for its land north of the main road between Swan Village and Great Bridge; and the next year William Street, between Charles Street

A Coronation Party at Fisher Street School 2 June 1953. Among the parents are June Pearson, Violet Aston and Lily Dunn. Around the table left to right are Maureen Wright, Doreen Tromans, Maureen Cash, Raymond Martin, Maureen Randle, Marion Martin, Edna Emms, Pat Emms, Pat Wright, Valerie Harman, Margaret Burton, Irene Randle, Barbara Cope, Celia Hill and Madeleine Hill. Thanks to Celia Asbury.

and Great Bridge Street, was described as newly laid out. Six years later, Fisher Street was noted at the top end of Great Bridge Street. It is probably named after James Fisher, who owned a tubes work in Great Bridge.

Although never a town in its own right, Great Bridge felt and looked like a town. From 1834, the Salem Church Great Bridge was meeting in Sheepwash Lane, and five years later its own chapel was ready for worship in that street. That year, 1839, the Great Bridge Congregational School began as an infants school. It operated until the 1860s, after which it focused upon a Sunday School. Additionally the Wesleyans were prominent locally with their own chapel by 1852.

With pubs and shops a plenty, and the Palace Picture House from 1912, Great Bridge was a self-contained place. It also boasted its own recreation space, Farley

Park off Whitehall Road, presented to the borough by Reuben Farley in 1891. It was a fitting gift, for Farley is the most famous child of Great Bridge. Born in 1826 in Whitehall Road on the West Bromwich side of Great Bridge, he was the son of a mining engineer who died when Farley was five. Little is known about how his mother made do as a widow at a time when you collared or clammed, but, according to the *Midland Chronicle*, "by hard work and that marked business ability which has distinguished all his undertakings' he became a successful coalmaster.

In 1861, still only in his thirties, he and his brother-in-law, George Taylor, bought a foundry and made a success of that undertaking. In the ensuing years, Farley also became chairman of Fellows, Moreton and Clayton, the biggest canal carriers in England; chairman of Edward Danks Ltd, the famous boilermakers of Oldbury; a director of the Hamstead Colliery Company; and an active force in the Sandwell Park Colliery.

These business achievements were matched by Farley's accomplishments in public life. He was typical of those powerful manufacturers and businessmen who believed passionately that they owed a due to the localities from which they gained

Inside the grocery shop of George Briscoe at 24c Market Place, Great Bridge, about 1953. This was the seventh Black Country branch of the firm. The staff are Gladys Hunt, May Steen and Mr Wood the manager. Thanks to Heather Whitehouse.

their wealth. If Bradford had Titus Salt, Manchester its John Bright and Birmingham its Joseph Chamberlain, then West Bromwich had Reuben Farley. From when he was a young man he "unceasingly identified himself with all the principal movements having for their object the progress and well being of the town and its inhabitants'.

These movements included the West Bromwich Building Society. Although he was not one of the founders of the society, he was one of the two men who audited the balance sheet which accompanied the earliest surviving document of the Society – its Second Annual Report (31 May 1851). Seven years later, he was made president and he held that office until he retired in 1897.

Farley's public activities were not restricted to the West Bromwich. He was a member of the Board of Guardians; a member of the first school board; and chairman of the Improvement Commissioners, the body which was the local authority before West Bromwich gained a town council. Under his leadership of the commissioners, West Bromwich obtained its own gas works and was provided with a Town Hall, Free Library, Market Hall and baths; and he also persuaded the Dartmouths to give to the town the park that bears their name. Unsurprisingly, when West Bromwich was incorporated in 1882, Farley was elected unanimously as

Samuel Pearson Ltd glass and bottle manufacturers, Charles Street in 1946. Standing at the side of the six bottle moulds are left to right Harry Arter, Harry Ralph and George Treadwell. Thanks to Jim Arter.

mayor. Indeed no other name was mooted. He continued to act vigorously on behalf of his fellow citizens, donating the land for Farley Park and bestowing the Oak House to the borough. In 1896, Farley was made the first freeman of West Bromwich. Mayor five times, when he died at the waning of the nineteenth century, the passing of 'Our Grand Old Man' was a blow for the whole of West Bromwich.

By an apt historical coincidence, another Great Bridge man born in Whitehall Road was the first mayor of the enlarged County Borough of West Bromwich in 1966, whereby Tipton and Wednesbury were brought together with West Bromwich. He was Joshua Churchman and it is fitting that a Great Bridge man held the highest office locally when both parts of Great Bridge were united for the first time under one local authority. For generations, Great Bridge was described in trades directories and other publications as part of Tipton. Today it is an integral part of Sandwell, but now as then Great Bridge retains its distinctiveness.

All the photos for this article are taken from Terry Price, Great Bridge Memories (Sutton Publishing). Terry Price is an indefatigable researcher of Great Bridge. A local man, he has devoted his life to bringing to the fore the history of Great Bridge and the lives of its people. He has done that job thoughtfully, sensitively and effectively. The author of two previous books on Great Bridge, Terry launched Great Bridge Memories at the Wesley Church in High Street, West Bromwich. Over 1,800 books were sold, a national record for Sutton Books.

As in the past, royalties from the book will be donated to: Great Bridge Methodist Church (with Hill Top Methodist Church); Hebron Hall, Horseley Heath; New Road Methodist Church; Ryders Green Methodist Church; Saint Paul's Church, Golds Hill; Saint Peter's Church, Great Bridge; and Toll End Methodist Church. The people of Great Bridge are fortunate to have such a determined historian and assiduous chronicler as Terry Price.

Chapter 17

FIRE CLAY AND BRICKS: HARRIS AND PEARSON

"What's in a name?" That's a question that is often posed, with the answer hopefully coming of, "A good name means a lot". But it's a question that can refer put not only to people but also to buildings. So what is in a building? Is any structure just there for functional purposes, having neither life nor soul. Or is a building something more, something infused with the spirits of those who have made it, worked in it or lived in it? If that is the case, then truly "A good building means a lot", for it is almost a living thing, brought to life by all those folk bonded with it and by the care that they have taken in its design, construction and upkeep.

Such a good building stands proud in Brettell Lane, Brierley Hill. It is the former offices of a great Black Country brickmaking concern, Harris and Pearson. Opened in 1888, the premises were made of bricks from local clay at the company's own works. There is a splendid variety of architectural ceramics in the façade, including both glazed and unglazed materials, and a wide range of colours. In particular, the white glazed lettering is a striking feature of the frontage and is a rare example of Victorian architectural graphics still in its original place.

Glazed brick walls exist in the entrance hall, landing and lobby, again in a breathtaking array of colours. The toilet also has glazed brick walls, but the outstanding feature internally is the mosaic tiles to the landing, lobby and in the small office on the first floor.

The Harris and Pearson Offices reflected the pride and success of a major local company, which traced its origins deep into the eighteenth century. In 1739 the Old Side Works was opened in Amblecote by the Earl of Stamford and Warrington. It was the first recorded example of a large purpose-built firebrick factory in the area and operated until 1928.

Along with coal, iron ore and limestone, fire clay was an essential perquisite both for the Industrial Revolution and for the emergence of the Black Country as one of the greatest manufacturing regions in the world. All furnaces and hearths had to be lined with firebricks to retain the heat, and the local clay was particularly suitable for a variety of uses, from Blast Furnaces to Glass Kilns. This clay was mined from local pits, being brought to the surface in slab form and 'weathered'.

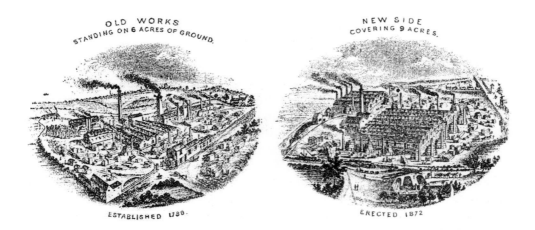

The works' engravings show the old and new works, of which the offices served the New Side one of 1872.

In 1852, the new partnership of Peter Harris and George Pearson acquired the lease of the six-acre Old Side Works then of six acres, and twenty years later increased the area to nine acres. During this period, the amount of fireclay extracted from the Staffordshire coalfields increased fivefold, and as the number of brick-making firms increased, so did Harris and Pearson grow. In 1872 they acquired from the Earl of Dudley the lease of an additional nine acres of land on which they built the New Side Works. It was bounded by the Stourbridge Canal to the west, Brettell Lane to the south, Bull Street to the north, and the Great Western Railway to the east. A few years later the two men purchased the freehold of this land and by the 1950s the business was producing about 17,000 tons of fireclay refractories per year.

Peter Harris died in 1874 followed by George Pearson in 1899, but the firm continued to be run by their descendants for many years. A number of other brick-makers were bought out and then in 1968 Dyson Group Plc. purchased the company, although it continued to trade independently until about 1980. Ten years later, the Harris and Pearson Offices were vacated - although the site itself continues to produce high temperature ceramics for the furnace industry operated by Dyson Industries Ltd. of Sheffield.

The Harris and Pearson Offices were identified as of special architectural and historic merit by Dudley Metropolitan Borough in March 1995. The Council wrote to the Department of National Heritage (now the Department for Culture, Media & Sport) to consider placing the building on the statutory list but no progress was made. The building was also placed on the draft of the "Local List".

A year later a concerned member of the public reported that scaffolding had appeared on the Harris & Pearson offices. There were fears that this magnificent building was to be demolished, for which no planning permission was needed. Because time was of the essence, Dudley Council took the unusual step of issuing a "Building Preservation Notice" to take immediate effect and which stopped further demolition. Fortunately, only part of the roof had been removed. This notice was valid for six months, and it gave English Heritage the time needed to look at the building and have it Grade II listed later in 1996.

In January 2003, the Harris and Pearson Offices were transferred to the West Midlands Buildings Trust. Later that year, a Heritage Lottery Fund Grant was approved of £627,000. Work to restore the buildings has been carried out by William Sapcote & Sons of Birmingham, a company with a fine reputation in this field. When completed, the Harris and Pearson buildings will be used again as offices.

Ensuring that restored buildings have a future life is a crucial aspect of the Trust's activities. As its name suggests, it is a Building Preservation Trust dedicated to the conservation of historic buildings in the West Midlands. It grew out of an initiative by the former West Midlands County Council, and was re-launched in 1990. Based in Stourbridge, it is run by a Council of Management. All Council members are volunteers and are elected by the membership, but most have expertise in the conservation field, and are experienced in dealing with historic buildings. In the past, the Trust has restored numbers 19-20, High Street, Kinver into a four-bed-roomed home; and a future project will see the restoration of Corngreaves Hall, a Grade 2 Listed Building in Cradley Heath.

As part of the Heritage Lottery Funded building restoration project, the West Midlands Historic Buildings Trust has commissioned Dr Paul Collins to carry out the oral history recordings. This will serve to put on record other recollections of people who worked at or were otherwise associated with Harris and Pearson. If you can help, please contact Dr Paul Collins at The West Midlands Historic Buildings Trust, Company Offices, Canal Street, Stourbridge, West Midlands, DY8 4LU. This is the same address for membership details of the Trust.

A Working Life at Harris and Pearson

Harry Smith now lives in Australia, but his memories of his working life at Harry and Pearson are vivid and he has written a fascinating account of the company, particularly in the late 1930s. It brings to the fore the importance of brickmaking, the interconnection between this process and the canals and railways, the ongoing significance of hand crafts, and the vital role played by women workers.

Harry writes: "My association with Harris & Pearson began in 1935,when, after leaving King Edward Grammar School Stourbridge, I was offered a position by Mr G. V. Evers of Pedmore, in one of the brickworks with which he was interested; ostensibly to study the manufacture and use of Refractories (firebricks as they were then called) and eventually to become a staff member.

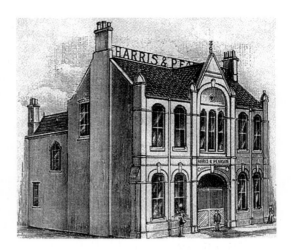

"I then joined Harris and Pearson, which was part of a group of companies – E.J & J Pearson, with their headquarters at the Delph in Brierley Hill, and from which we were controlled. As far as I can gather, Harris & Pearson was in the process of restarting; (following a period of depression), and taking on more employees, and I found myself entering the portal of what

The pen drawing of the Harris and Pearson offices that appeared in the 'Black Country and its Industries' catalogue in 1904.

was to me, the gateway to an industry which was to become the most satisfying and interesting of my working life and was eventually to bring me to Australia.

"The main office was an imposing two-story building. As one entered from Brettell Lane, the office ground floor left, was the Works Office, and abode of Mr Charlie Salt the Works Foreman, and the office at right was the Sales Office – the occupant at this time being Mr Smallman. The main feature as far as I was concerned was the Time Clock, which was at the right hand end and had a distinctive ring. The first floor was taken up by (at left) the office of Mr Pearson (Ronnie) The Works Manager – (and I believe one of the original Pearson family), and the remaining office was the Administration Centre. After an exhaustive interview with Mr Salt, I was told that I was to begin my education in the Carpenters Shop.

"The main clay used at that time was the famous Stourbridge Old Mine Clay - however that was fast running out, and was being replaced by New Mine Clay, which was not as refractory. Clay was obtained from Withymoor. There were two grinding pans, one was the original and was driven by a coal fired boiler, which provided steam for an old marine engine, which in turn drove a system of driving belts, this marine engine had a huge flywheel which constantly needed chocking up and was the cause of many stoppages.

"The second pan had an electric motor drive and was the more efficient of the two. These two mills provided feed for the two Pug Mills (extruders) via tempering tubs in which the ground clay was watered down to become plastic; some quite stiff for extruders, and some quite soft for the hand moulders.

"Most processes were labour intensive and forklifts etc were unheard of. The extruders were housed in long sheds (stoves) and were serviced by men with special long topped barrows who would run down the stove and stack the bricks for drying. The extruders made mainly bricks of 9x4½x3 dimensions and by the use of wires could be made to produce Side Arch and End Arch etc.

"The extruders could also make large stiff clots for use with the presses. These were again hand operated and were known as 'Swing Presses' or 'Hand Presses'. The Swing Presses consisted of a heavy screw some 4" to 6" in diameter attached to a large circular wheel. By turning the wheel the press would move up and down. The operator (sometimes 2) stood on a platform and swung the heavy wheel, and the screw drove the top plate into the die box and pressed the bricks. Accidents were prone to happen for the press had very few safety features.

"The other method of manufacture was by hand moulding, which is where I came in. Since the advent of Plastic Refractories had not yet arrived; most specially shaped bricks were made in wooden moulds; by both male and female moulders. These moulds could be quite complicated and necessitate either loose fittings in a timber frame or collapsible moulds.

A cracking shot of a charabanc outing of Harris and Pearson workers in the 1920s.

"At one time three of us could not keep up with demand and we had to send for a Mould and Pattern Maker from Amblecote Works. The moulds could be very large as in the case of glass house tank blocks (which necessitated two moulders to handle one) or very small which normally women would make. One such lady was Nell Coleman who would make a day's tally with the best of them and nine times out of ten, she would finish before them, and, at the time, she was reputed to be almost 70 years old!

"The men made the larger and more complicated shapes and foremost among them were the Timmins Family who also had a Fish and Chip Shop in (I think) the Delph. It was always possible to tell which moulder made which brick.

"When I first started in the Carpenters Shop, my boss was an ex-Delph man, Ted Pitt, who was a first class craftsman but was on the verge of retirement; he was succeeded by George Westwood another of the same ilk. During my time here, I attended Stourbridge Tech School and studied Engineering Drawing and Science, together with as much information on Firebricks as the Library could offer.

"The bricks in the most part were dried in what were called "Stoves" and these were heated by means of flues running the entire length of the floor, and fed from fire boxes at the end. The area immediately above the fire box had a double thickness of brick, for the heat generated by the coal fire was considerable and this area was used to ensure that larger bricks were completely dried out. Unfortunately at one Christmas Party, one of the setters (male) fell asleep on this particular floor and as a result was fairly well burned.

"Firing of the dried brick was done in round Down Draft Kilns or the new 'Belgian' Continuous Kiln, which had been completed just before I arrived, and was the first step in modernisation of the plant. All kilns were coal fired by hand but the 'Belgian' had the advantage of never stopping for setting or discharging.

"All setting, except that of gas retorts (which required special handling by a separate gang due to their size and shape) was done by women carriers, in charge of a male setter. These women wore a large padded bustle around their waist on which they would rest the dried brick, ready for the setter to place in situ. Some of the distances walked by these women, and the weight they carried would tax the strength of a man – no wonder that one would not answer them back or make suggestive remarks!! But they kept at it all day and seemed to thrive on it – the head setter Billy Mailley must certainly have had a way with him.

"The factory was well placed for the ingress and egress of raw materials and finished product, having the canal (cut) on one side, and the railway siding on the other, with Brettell Lane at the front for use of road transport. One of my most disliked jobs was to have to 'block off' railway trucks to prevent the load of bricks from moving. Inevitably by the time it had been shunted about half a dozen times, it had shifted, and my excuse was that the 'nails were not long enough' did not seem to wash at all well!!

"Which brings me to relate the story of my first ever job at Harris & Pearson: - Ted Pitt, having looked me over said 'I've just the job for you, take this hammer and report to Ronnie Pearson's office and Charlie Salt will tell you what to do'. I did so, and was given a handful of tacks, and told to go to Mr Pearson's office and tack the lino down. Since Mr Pearson was in his office, I had to work around his desk and I thought this most unbecoming for a grammar school boy – 'was this what higher education was all about?'

"The foregoing was all about work at Harris & Pearson pre World War Two. As far as I was concerned it came to an end in 1939 (September) in this fashion: - On this particular Sunday myself and George Westwood were working overtime to get out some moulds needed for (as I remember) a large coke oven order. I was en route from the carpenter's shop to the stove to check out sizes and fit etc of a fairly large mould, when George shouted that war had been declared. I forthwith dropped the mould in the middle of the yard; said good day to George, grabbed my bike and headed home. Next day (Monday) I joined the R.A.F. – I have often wondered who picked up, or fell over, that mould – never found out!

The Harris and Pearson building after restoration.

"I returned in February 1946 and obviously great changes had been made during my absence. The progress made necessary for higher quality refractories had resulted in the demand for brick made of the lower grade Stourbridge New Mine Clay having to be bolstered by the importation of Castle Carey Higher Alumina Clay for the production of stiff plastic material.

"With production of higher refractories, new methods of production were introduced, one of which was the introduction of the 'Slip Casting Method'. This was under the control of Mr S.C. Waterton with whom I worked in the manufacture of the new type of mould required for this type of production. Slip Casting also required new plant, and accordingly a new mixer and blunger were installed, and more stringent quality control was introduced.

"The higher alumina product made; obviously required higher firing and more control over heating and cooling and so a new gas fired kiln (reputed to be able to fire to 1400°C) was built. Since Slip Cast Blocks were used in the local glass industry, and the method of building glass smelting tanks required them to be almost joint free, great accuracy in block dimensions was of maximum priority, and so the old existing grinding machine was updated to accommodate the new harder blocks.

"However, technology had made such great advances during the war that refractory requirements were entirely different and higher quality, and speed of installation was the norm. Gone were the Low Alumina Bricks, they were rapidly being replaced by the new castable and mouldable refractories, which by their very existence spelt the death knell to old time installation, which required special shapes and lots of jointing and was labour intensive.

"It was obvious to me that the industry was in decline when E.J & J Pearson built a small plant on the opposite side of Brettell Lane, (basically adjacent to Rutter Bros foundry) for production of the new breed of refractories. I therefore decided that it was time to look for fresh fields and pastures new. For a short time I obtained a job at George King Harrison in charge of production.

"During the war, my squadron had many Australians, and listening to their banter, and often serious talk, I gradually came to think that here was the opportunity for which I was looking !! After talking it over with my wife we decided to make the break and I obtained a position in Queensland, but on arrival in Adelaide, I was approached by a representative of Adelaide Potteries with an offer I could not refuse – that of developing a viable refractory industry in South Australia!! 1952 was a very good year for my family and me. But that is another story ..."

Chapter 18

ESCAPE FROM GERMANY: THE CHAINMAKERS OF BRIERLEY HILL

Pat Woolley of Derwent Close, Pensnett, and originally from Chapel Street, Brierley Hill, has uncovered a fascinating family story to do with relations on her mom's side Nocks of Brierley Hill. It all came about because an American lady was looking for information on those Nocks who emigrated to the United States in 1903. She is Gladys Runkel of Jonestown, Pennsylvania, who is now eighty years old. Gladys is the granddaughter of a Titus Nock, whilst Pat is descended from a Ben Nock. They are still trying to work out the exact relationship between the two men but in doing so they have brought to the fore a story that would have remained hidden without their investigations.

After contacting Gladys, Pat delved into the local papers for the early twentieth century. It seems that "Titus Nock and his brother John were born at a place called Shepherd's Fold in Blackheath into a family of nailers. In the 1890s Titus and John came to live in Brierley Hill. Both men were chainmakers at the Round Oak. Titus met and married a Brierley Hill girl from Albion Street named Harriet Beddall. They married at Saint Michael's Church. John married Jane Shakespeare, also from Brierley Hill.

"In 1903 Titus and John decided to try for a better life in the USA but came back in 1904-05. In 1906 a party of Germans visiting Round Oaks steelworks were impressed by the chainmaking skills of these men and offered them well-paid jobs in Germany. Tempted with the offer of a better wage and standard of living they decided to go. This caused a lot of panic and a Mr Stitch was sent to Germany to fetch them back. They were smuggled back into the country before any damage was done to the chainmaking industry.

"Titus was now living at 22, Brickiln Street, Brierley Hill but tragedy struck the family. Two of his little girls died from measles on the same day in 1909. Daisy was aged two and Lily was four. After this they decided to go to the USA again – Titus, John, their wives and children all sailing off for a better life. Again tragedy was to hit Titus's family with the loss of two young sons.

"Titus and John themselves carried on at a steelworks in Lebanon in Pennsylvania. In the 1930s Titus built a hotel and they brewed their own beer. Then Titus and his son-in-law, Flotd Pittenger (the father of Gladys), built small homes which they rented out. From then they never looked back."

Pat has kindly sent me copies of the press cuttings which tell of the remarkable events concerning Titus and John in 1906. They are taken from *The County Express*. The first was headlined "Germany and the Chain Trade. Expert Workmen Enticed to the Continent". It declared that "some sensation has been caused by the news that two chainmakers and four strikers employed at the Earl of Dudley's Round Oak Works have left for Germany, having been presumably been enticed by that country by the promise of a much higher rate of pay ..."

Harriet and Titus Nock in America.

The correspondent explained that the emigration of a few workmen "in the ordinary course of affairs is not a matter of moment, but in this instance the men are specially skilled in large chainmaking". Indeed, the chainmaking district of the Black Country was supreme in heavy chain and there "are not as many men making large cables in the whole of America as there are in the ordinary sized English works". Much of the Black Country chain was exported to Germany and consequently the emigration of the men "becomes a matter of importance, and is viewed with seriousness, not only by the employers whom they have left, but also by the trade union to which they belonged".

Having gone without even telling their employers, the six men were back in England within a fortnight. They were accompanied by Thomas Stitch, the general secretary of the Chainmakers' Association of Unity Villa, Cradley Heath and a member of the Rowley Regis Urban District Council; and Mr Fellows junior, son of John Fellows, a prominent chain manufacturer. A week later, *The County Express* was able to bring to its readers "The Full Story of How Germany Made a Bid for the Cable Trade".

It is difficult today to understand the deep concern about the loss of "British secrets", but then Germany was regarded with fear as a large, populous country that was determined to make itself an industrial power and claim for itself "a place in the sun" as an imperial nation. A new state that had emerged in the 1880s after decades of expansion by the militaristic Prussians, Germany was feared by France and was viewed uneasily by Britain because of its resolve to challenge British naval supremacy and trading dominance.

For several years, tension had been rising between Germany and Britain. In 1896 there were anti-German riots caused by the support of Kaiser Wilhelm II for the Boers of South Africa, who then had their own republics; and five years later Joseph Chamberlain, the famed MP for Birmingham who had such wide support in the West Midlands, delivered a speech on world affairs that was regarded by the Germans as hostile to them. Then in 1905, with Germany rapidly building new warships, Admiral Fisher requested the Admiralty to draft contingency plans in case France was attacked.

The next year, during which the chainmakers were "enticed" away, the British launched the HMS "Dreadnought", which was the most awesome battleship in the world, and Edward VII and the Kaiser met to try and ease the worsening Anglo-German relations.

The reporter for *The County Express* understood the wider picture. He emphasised that "most of the other trades upon which England could years ago pride herself as standing in the foremost rank have either been very successfully copied by other nations or have been carried away root and branch to swell the industrial activities of foreign countries". By contrast the cable trade was an English monopoly and it gained even more significance because it was an essential aspect of British shipbuilding, an industry vital to the maintenance of British naval might.

Thus Titus Nock and his fellows were unwittingly drawn into a dangerous diplomatic game of brag, in which Britain and Germany strove to outdo each other with their hand. Their adventures had begun after Titus and Thomas Ellis, another chainmaker, had noticed an advertisement for men of their trade at a chain and rolling mills in Duisburg on the Rhine. They wrote for more details, "not dreaming", as Thomas put it, "that anything would turn up, certainly nothing like what has since transpired".

A week or so later a representative of the German firm arrived at Round Oak, along with a man from Leeds who acted as an interpreter. After some discussion, Titus and Thomas remained unconvinced about taking up a new job abroad, but the next day the two representatives returned and this time nothing was left undone to induce the Black Country chaps "to consent to take very lucrative positions at Duisburg; no promise was too great, no desire that the men could think of was unconceded; they were desperate in securing the transfer of the Englishmen and their strikers". In the end, Titus and Thomas agreed to move, along with their strikers John Harris, George Kendall, Sidney Newton and John Nock and three other men.

Their departure was secret, although Thomas Stitch soon found out about it. He rushed to Birmingham and persuaded three of men to stay, but the other six had gone on the day before. They made their way to Flushing in the Netherlands and thence by first-class passage to Dusiburg, where they were boarded in a prominent restaurant. Treated like lords, the men were looked after and "guarded" by a fellow called Augustine, who had been "specially sent for from Austria".

They were given a month to assist in the making of their tools and on one occasion the Englishmen "gave an exhibition of their skill in cable making. Three sample links were made, and when, after a very sever test, many tons beyond what was deemed beyond the breaking strain, the link broke separate from the 'shut', the delight of the firm's managing director and high government officials, who were specially invited to witness the event, was so great that the six men were soon afterwards seated go dinner on the lawn of the managing director's house" and were lavishly entertained with hock.

To their surprise, the Black Country exiles were then visited by Thomas Stitch, and Robert Oliver, foreman of the Round Oak chain works department. Stitch had the support of George Hatton, manager of the Earl of Dudley's Round Oak Iron, Steel and Chain Works, and Sir George Hingley of Noah Hingley and Sons. They were told that their old jobs were still open to them and that they had a duty to their country by coming home. Nonetheless, they declined to do so, apparently because of the rewards that they had been promised.

Checking the chain at Hingley's in the early 1920s.

Chainmakers at work.

These included high payment by the hundredweight; return trips to England twice a year paid for by their employers; holiday pay – a thing almost unknown in this country; sick pay at the rate of two thirds their wages, another major benefit; and a "a lot of money", £50 each, at the end of their twelve months' engagement. This was a substantial sum for a working man. An unskilled man would be lucky to earn that in a year, and it was twice as much as women could earn in backbreaking work in the brickfields and chain shops.

Another provision made by the German employers for their workers was that of a canteen. This was reported as a "strange" feature. It opened for an hour at a time for several times in the day, and served beer and coffee at "remarkably cheap" rates. What was more "a servant of the firm did nothing except supply the demands of the workers and keeping the place".

With high wages, good facilities, excellent lodgings and the appeal of holiday and sickness pay, it is little wonder that the Black Country men were attracted to a year's work in Germany. Their English employers lagged well behind their German counterparts in providing for the welfare of their employees, and most would continue to do so for a number of years.

Back in the West Midlands, Thomas Stitch wrote two letters to the men. He realised that the positive aspects of employment in Germany were bought at a high price. German society as a whole was dominated by the military and the nobility and trade unionism was weak whilst trade unionists on strike were often attacked by the police. He pointed this out to the men, and stressed that they were in danger of severing their connections with their union. This last argument was a strong one to men attached to their trade association.

Moreover, Stitch went on, "there was no doubt that after they had been there a few months, and all that was promised them fulfilled for that length of time, they would be absolutely at the mercy of the German manufacturers. Then they would be without the assistance which their strong organisation in England could otherwise render."

After careful consideration of the points made by Stitch, the men heeded him. They were also affected by reports on the affair in local newspapers that had been sent to them by their relatives. In response, they sent Stitch a cablegramme announcing their decision to return home. Still, "the difficulties in the way of getting the men from Germany seemed insurmountable".

Stitch resolved to go back. He was joined by Sidney Fellows, who spoke German. By now the movements of the six men were watched closely, and Stitch and Fellows realised that they could not go to the works or the restaurant to speak with their countrymen. Leaving their base some miles away, they split up. Fellows went to the restaurant posing as a German and after the strikers left for work, he held a German newspaper and followed them. Arousing no suspicion he managed to slip a note to John Harris, unbeknownst to Augustine, who watched over them. As he did so, Fellows whispered, "From Tom Stitch."

The strikers handed the message to Nock and Ellis. It indicated that they should meet Stitch and Fellows at an appointed time at the railway station. After a discussion, they determined to do so. But it was almost an impossibility to get away from Augustine, the interpreter. So Nock and Ellis agreed to grumble at the supper table that the strikers were late for the meal. In the meantime, their four companions went upstairs to change their clothes "and thereby give colour to the

Chainmakers at work at Hingley's in the early 1920s. Thanks to the Sandwell Society of Film Makers.

excuse for the grumbles". Expressing annoyance, Nock and Ellis told the restaurant keeper they were going for a walk whilst they waited. Leaving the building they made their way quickly to the railway station, where they boarded a train with Stitch.

The strikers had more difficulty in escaping, but did so after persuading the interpreter to have a little too much to drink. In need of a nap, he went upstairs to his room, into which he was locked. The strikers then split up. Harris and Newton went off, followed by Newton and John Nock, who "soon discovered they wee in a quandary, for neither of them knew the way to the station which was approaching two miles distant".

Meeting a German, they attempted to ask him the whereabouts of the station but could not make themselves understood. Luckily, Newton had a piece of paper and John Nock a blacklead pencil and so they drew an engine, with smoke coming out of the "puffer", and a carriage. The German recognised what they were seeking and took them to their destination.

Meeting Fellows there, they caught a train and met up with the other party, before boarding another train to Flushing, in The Netherlands – whence they embarked on a ship for England, having "the satisfaction of having very smartly outwitted the Germans".

Stitch proved an able general secretary in more ways than one. He secured for the men their former jobs and took the sting out of criticism by paying them tribute. He declared that they deserved a good word because they had put aside financial gain as they did not want to seriously injure either the chain trade or their union. They set at nought their own interests and in making good their escape left behind all possessions they had taken with them.

I congratulate Pat Woolley on digging out this captivating episode in the history of the Black Country and chainmaking. It is rare that the lives of individual working-class people made their way into the papers and this makes the story of Titus Nock and his fellows even more valuable historically. Unfortunately, the growing rivalry between Britain and Germany did not abate and in 1914 the two countries blundered into a bloody conflict that would destroy millions of lives. By then Titus and John Nock were in America, Does anyone know what happened to the other four men?

Chapter 19

A PROPER BLACK COUNTRY MON: JACK HUMPHRIES

Ian Hammond now lives in Cannock, but was born in Harden, Walsall. He moved to Cannock when he was ten after his Dad got a job at Littleton Pit. Growing up in the 1960s and 70s, Ian remembers that "I used to love talking to me Grandad about the coal mines and local history and in 1982 I taped him so I would have a record. We were sat at my Uncle Ray's house in Bloxwich and my Grandma sat with us occasionally talking in the background. In 1969 my Grandad contracted TB after already suffering from dust on the chest from the pit (he continually coughs painfully through the tape) and he went into Goscote Hospital (the former dreaded Walsall workhouse). He fought on and he lived until September 1988, and died just short of his 60th wedding anniversary. My Grandma, born in 1907 died shortly after reaching 90. Tough people from hard times and we must not forget them. My son is called Jack. I just wish I had more tapes of all my grandparents!"

Ian's Grandad was the son of John Humphries senior, who had walked from his home in Radnorshire in the later years of Queen Victoria's reign to find work in the Black Country. He followed a long line of Welshmen and women who had made that same long treck. By the sixteenth century, and probably for many years before, cattlemen from Wales were driving their beasts across the Severn and eastwards to fatten up and sell in the west midlands at markets such as Walsall, founded in 1219; Wolverhampton, where market traders were gathering from at least 1204; Dudley, where there seems to have been a market from 1268; and Birmingham, where the market started in 1166. Indeed, so important were the Welsh dealers and their trading connection with the west midlands that one end of the Beast Market in Birmingham's High Street was called the Welsh Cross.

Elsewhere, the wealthy Goughs of Wolverhampton traced their origins, according to Robert K. Dent and Joseph Hill, to the "martial Gochs of the Principality—ancestors of Owen Glendower and the brave Sir Matthew Gough, who fought under Talbot, and a goodly line of Wolverhampton wool-staplers". Making their money through dealing in wool at a time when Wolverhampton was a major centre of that trade, the Goughs invested their money in land, buying part of Perry Barr and then becoming lords of Edgbaston in Birmingham. Their descendants still own much of that valuable district.

Another successful Welsh family was that of the Lloyds. On the male side they claimed to descend from Aled, who in the eleventh century was a king of Dyfed – the later shires of Cardigan, Pembroke and Carmarthen. The family came to Dolobran in Montgomeryshire about 1300 and took the name of Lloyd in the later fifteenth century. Two hundred years later, Charles Lloyd the second became a Quaker, as did his son, Sampson, who came to Birmingham in 1698. He did so because he and his father had been persecuted for their religious beliefs and he felt that there would be more tolerance in Birmingham, where religious dissent was more accepted.

Sampson's grandson, Sampson Lloyd the third, was instrumental in setting up Taylor and Lloyd's Bank in 1765 (later Lloyd's Bank). He also came into the ownership of mines in Wednesbury through the inheritance of his mother, Sarah Parkes, a member of a prominent local family. Sampson's own grandson, Samuel the second, went to live in Wednesbury in 1818 to take charge of the family's affairs there. Thenceforth, the Lloyds also moved into blast furnaces and engineering in the concern of Lloyd's, Foster's and Co. However, in the early 1860s, the financial position of the company was strained badly after it was not paid for ironwork that it had supplied to the firm constructing the Blackfriars Bridge over the Thames in London. With the huge loss of a quarter of a million pounds, the business had to be sold to the Patent Shaft and Axeltree Company Limited, also of Wednesbury.

Undaunted by this setback, Samuel Lloyd the third established other iron businesses in Wednesbury, in which his sons became involved. The most famous of these was F. H. Lloyd's. Named after Francis Henry, this steelfounders was in Myvod Road, which recalls with English spelling the village of Meifod that was close to Dolobran, the ancestral home of the Lloyd's in Montgomeryshire. In fact Francis Henry Lloyd lived in Dolobran House on Woodgreen Road. It later became part of West Bromwich Technical College and was then knocked down.

The great majority of the Welsh who came to our region did not become as rich as the Lloyds and Goughs. For hundreds of years, and like John Humphries, most of them were working people and they came from mid-Wales, from Brecon and Radnorshire – counties lying directly to our west. Then from the 1920s great numbers of men and women from South Wales came to the Black Country, seeking work as the mines closed in The Valleys. Their impact has been important and wide-ranging, from industry to teaching, but unfortunately it has been overlooked.

John Humphries himself married Ruth, from a family in Shelfield. It is believed that she or one of her sisters, Mary-Ann and Lily, worked in a room that did sewing for Queen Victoria. Their mother and father, Sarah and Joseph Chater, lived in a cottage and Joseph traipsed the streets with a hand cart selling pies made by his family. As for Jack, he was born on 3 September 1905 in that Hamstead south of the River Tame and which was part of Handsworth and not West Bromwich. The family must have moved when he was little as he grew up in Shelfield, and his dad worked down the pits at Aldridge.

The first job that the young Jack Humphries had was with his grandfather, helping out with his pie cart. Afterwards Jack started work at John Boy's timberyard on Pleck Road, Walsall. He was there for about three or four months and then went down the mine at Hamstead Colliery, grafting on eight hour shifts, six days a week for round about £2 a week. As for holidays, "you used to get three days at Easter without pay, three days Whitsuntide, August, Christmas, no pay".

There was no training and at first Jack "was minding a door, what they call door minding". He stayed at Hamstead for a few years and "came to Aldridge in 1922 and I worked at Aldridge till 1936 and it closed and I never worked on the face at Aldridge. When Aldridge finished I went to Walsall Wood colliery and I worked on the face there and I was there for about two years till 1938. Went to Hamstead colliery in 1938 and went on the face and sort of got different jobs during the time I was there."

Sarah and Joseph Chater, Jack's maternal grandparents outside their cottage in Shelfield. Notice Joseph's hand cart, from which he sold pies, and that Sarah is wearing a man's flat cap – as did many older working-class women.

At Aldridge Colliery there was the six foot seam and "you could stand up and there was the Deep and the Shallow. You could stand up in that. Now at Hamstead Colliery there was the Thick Coal. In the Thick Coal area roundabout 20 or 30 foot thick coal at Hamstead and they used to have to do it in layers, what they call the thick coal."

There were several faces at Hamstead, called districts, and they were "a good way off ... They had what they used to call the paddy run. It used to take the men to within a certain distance of the face what they called the paddy trucks that the men used to ride on, electrically driven". It was about a twenty minute walk to reach the coal itself. At Aldridge the face was not so far and was within walking distance and they used to get at the coal "more or less with a pike, pick and shovel, no conveyor belts and there was no coal cutters it was all done be the hand".

As a youngster Jack was involved in two strikes, in 1921 and 1926, the time of the General Strike. The 1920s and 1930s were hard days for miners. Despite the terrible loss of life in the First World War, an optimistic feeling swept the land with the coming of peace in 1918. All working men aged over 21 were at last granted the right to vote and Lloyd George and other politicians promised to build a Land Fit for Heroes. Those high hopes were dashed in the severe economic downturn that followed the brief post-war boom. Britain's staple industries were most badly hit. Amongst them was mining.

Having expanded rapidly in the later nineteenth century, mining now started to fall back. During the war, the Government had taken increased control over mining, and in 1919 a Commission recommended the nationalization of mines and coal royalties. This call was ignored, although working hours were limited to seven a day. For a time, coal exports remained high, as did prices, but in 1921 Government control ended, along with controlled wages. Transport workers and railwaymen threatened to back the miners in a Triple Alliance, but this failed on 15 April, 'Black Friday'. Left on their own, the miners had to end their strike on the stringent terms of the owners.

Ruth Humphries, Jack's mother, with her sisters Mary-Anne Penn and Lily, and perhaps, Jim – Jack's brother.

The main road through Shelfield in the early 1900s, with the tram lines in place.

Conditions for miners continued to deteriorate. British coal began to lose its export markets and with a stagnant demand at home, there was less need for as much coal as had been produced in the past. Unhappily, the return to the gold standard for sterling meant that the value of the pound was increased, so making it even more expensive to export British coal. The problems of mining were exacerbated by a lack both of investment and an overall strategy. Many mines were small-scale concerns and were unable to afford modern machinery. Consequently, they could not compete with large mines abroad that had brought in mechanization.

By 1925, mine owners were seeking to cut costs by demanding that miners work for less money for longer hours. After a lock out of the miners by the bosses, the Triple Alliance and the General Council of the TUC strongly supported the workers and the Conservative Government was forced to make concessions on the so-called Red Friday by agreeing to a nine month subsidy to maintain wages and profits. The Samuel Commission was set up and when it reported it rejected nationalization and recommended the end of the subsidy as well as cuts in wages so as to maintain profitability for owners.

Mine owners followed this with the publication of new terms for miners. Amongst them were an extension of the seven-hour working day, district wage-agreements, and a reduction in the wages. Depending on various factors, wages would be cut by between 10% and 25%. The mine owners declared that if the miners did not accept the new terms then from 1 May 1926 they would be locked out of the pits. That is what happened. The unbridgeable divide between miners and their employers led to a lock out and national strike.

That day a TUC Conference resolved to back the miners and a General Strike was called from 3 May to force the Government into negotiations. It was an objective that could not be attained. Both the Government and the mine owners had been taken advantage of the preceding nine months to strengthen their position. Plans had been put in place to maintain of supplies and keep the country on the move, and the armed forces and volunteers took on the duties of many transport workers. The General Strike collapsed after nine days. The TUC strove in vain to get the Government to state that strikers who went back to work would not be victimized. The reply was as unfeeling as flint: the Government had "no power to compel employers to take back every man who had been on strike.

Once again the miners were left to fight an unwinnable battle on their own. Many doggedly held out for months, but with nothing coming in stomachs ached and bodies weakened. Jack recalled those hungry days all too well: "Well I was out for about six months. They kept drifting back 'cos they sort of lost the strike and we was gradually drifting back one at a time. Less money then when we come out, not more like you get now. Well as for food it was more or less left to the goodness of the people the shopkeepers who let you have it on credit that's how we carried on. Me being single I hadn't more or less got the responsibility.

"We used to go coal picking on the pit banks and some of 'em used to go digging for coal at Bentley 'cos there were what they call a seam of coal at Bentley Common what they call outcrop. Well there's all houses built there now, Bentley, and they used to go and get it, gang of men get it, dig down about nine or ten feet and get it out. Outcrop. They used to sell it to the factory and got money."

Across the Black Country, miners and their women and children, desperate for fuel, picked around in the totty bonks

The wedding of Annie Elizabeth Lefevre and Jack Humphries on 20 May 1929 at Saint Peter's Church of England, Stafford Street, Walsall. Also shown are Walter, Annie's brother, and Elise Penn, Jack's cousin.

Annie and Jack Humphries on 22 October 1950.

looking for bits and pieces of coal. With hardly anything coming in, many a person was clammed and as time went on it was more and more difficult to get food on the slate (credit). Starved back into work, as Jack remembered, the miners had to accept less money and longer hours. Sadly, many of them never worked again. There were not the jobs available as there had been in the high days of mining, whilst those who had been active in the Miners Union were blacked as gaffers took the opportunity to force out workers they did not want.

Three years after the General Strike, on 20 May 1929 Jack married his sweetheart, Annie Elizabeth Lefevre at Saint Peter's Church of England, Stafford Street, Walsall. After a couple or three months living with his father in Shelfield, the couple returned to Walsall in lodgings and "it was nearly 1932 before we managed to get a cottage of our own down Stubbers Green, right by Stubbers Green Pool, Dumble Derry Lane. The cottage the first house we had the water was on we had water laid on." Annie, Jack's wife, noted that "there was one up, one down and a landing sort of thing which you could use as a small bedroom, but there was no door."

Then in 1936, Jack came back to Hamstead Colliery. He brought to mind that there were two or three accidents a year at there, not due to water at but "more or less explosions due to the pressure of the strata". However, he was involved in "one in very bad one in 1940 ... I was in an explosion and got buried in an

159

explosion. Not completely buried, more or less trapped by the timber but I was fast for four and half hours before I got freed.

"Well, it's a funny sensation when the explosion comes due to pressure what they used to call bumps and I was driving a pony at the time. The pony was killed but I didn't lose consciousness and eventually after a bit they found me and all they done was to get me out which they did after about four and half hours. They took me to the Manor Hospital and I was in there about eight weeks. It was me legs, it sort of done something to the muscles and sinews of the legs. Anyway it eventually got better and I went back down the pit again."

Reflecting on his working life and bearing in mind it was over twenty years ago when he was talking and when we still had a mining industry, Jack "wouldn't say they was good old days because nowadays if a chap or boy wants to go in the mines he goes to training mine. When I first went down the mine, I went down the mine and I got to find my own way in, there was no training facilities in them days not like you got the training. You got a colliery over the Chase for training. There wasn't even electric light down the pit. They used to call 'em the good old days, but I wouldn't like to see 'em again."

This article is dedicated to a proper Black Country mon, Jack Humphries, 1905-1988, and to his family.